Road Map to Power

Syed Arshad Husain, M.D.
&
A. Darius Husain

self-help general
self-help personal growth happiness
philosophy general

Dedication

To our Jennifers, the best of travel companions.
For Ava and Danny, the reasons for taking the journey.

Contents

Syed Arshad Husain, M.D. & A. Darius Husain

The 10 Rules of Power

1) You are likely average, mathematically speaking.

2) We have become more Wal-Mart than Wildebeest.

3) When you get to the part about "created equal," keep reading.

4) Governments cannot legislate genetics.

5) Looking for security? It's in the attachment.

6) Chances are you're happy (despite the best efforts of the media).

7) Forge your armor out of resiliency.

8) If you don't like the ending, rewrite the story.

9) Cultivate your garden.

10) Be more than humane, be a humanitarian.

Syed Arshad Husain, M.D. & A. Darius Husain

1

The Normal Distribution

Rule of the Road: You're likely average,
mathematically speaking.

Mile Markers: August in Missouri, Cash Only, Projection, Revelation, Bell Curve, Standard Deviation, The 99%, Normal Distribution, Wealth, Pareto Curve, The 1%, Power Paradigm, Road Map to Power

I am about to tell you a secret. Once it's told, you must promise me that you won't stop reading. Here it is: There is a high probability that you are average. I know this revelation is probably the worst news you could receive outside of learning that you have been diagnosed with a terminal disease. No one wants to be thought of as average. To be fair, you are likely above average because you prefer to invest in books that heighten self-awareness rather than splurge on convenience store romance novels. Let me rephrase, then: No one will accuse you of being elite. Before I permanently offend you when we haven't even had a chance to get to know each other, why don't we take a step back.

This book is written for people whom society labels as average and refuses to consider as elite. They have neither the family fortune nor the biological endowment that would enable them to achieve power as it is modernly defined. This group constitutes the overwhelming majority of any community. They may openly reject or suffer silently in a culture that values celebrity and materialism and therefore favors the few who can muster seemingly unlimited resources. Its aim is to promote a sense of respect for these individuals' lives and affairs, allowing them to wield an authentic power that can lead to personal satisfaction.

Although this book has been a lifetime in the making, its evolution gained momentum during a chance encounter. The experience would plant a seed of questioning that would preoccupy my mind and challenge what I had convinced myself to be true.

This story begins modestly, save for an overwhelming heat. August in Missouri is a devastating formula of 100-degree temperatures and hot, wet winds traveling up the Gulfstream. A stretch of black parking lot trapped my vehicle, glistening golden in the sun, my means home after ten hours of hard work. As I opened the door, I braced myself for the wave of humidity that fills a car baked in the heat. Situating myself in the driver's seat, I felt suffocated. Relief would only come from the turning of the key, the starting of the ignition, and the eventual sweet breeze of the air conditioner. However, the car wouldn't start. I turned the key over and over again and was barely rewarded with a slight hum.

Every day since I accepted my position as the director of a newly built psychiatric treatment center for children and adolescents, I have driven 30 miles each way from my home in Columbia to the small town of Fulton, Missouri. This journey was common among the employees of the hospital that preferred the more urban, not quite metropolitan, feel of the college town over the isolated, if not tranquil, scene of central Missouri. This daily drive was part of the justification for splurging on the gold Audi 5000. Now this car was failing me despite the efforts of a gathering number of colleagues attempting a jump start.

As I was contemplating my shrinking options, a voice cut through the thick air. "Well, Dr. Husain, looks like I'll be taking you back to Columbia."

His name was Bob (not his real name), a mental health worker with whom I had collaborated previously and whom I had always naturally liked. Bob was also a resident of Columbia and a fellow traveler. His offer was especially enticing considering the alternative: calling my wife, asking her to make the 60-mile round trip, and spending 30 miles of it hearing the many reasons she knew buying this car was a terrible idea.

It was at that moment that I first noticed his automobile. Bob's two-door Toyota Tercel was splattered with rust holes that resembled coffee stains on a bleached white napkin. Stepping down into the passenger side,

I caught a glimpse of a weathered dashboard with noticeable cracks forming. Despite the obvious physical blemishes, the interior of the car was extremely clean and judging by the long list of digits on the odometer, obviously well cared for. Besides, I was no stranger to "rough" accommodations, having experienced refugee camps at age eight, sharing a living space with ten siblings in Karachi, Pakistan, and more recently, being a penniless medical intern in Harlem. I may have embraced more luxuries in this current chapter of my life, but memories of a more simple existence were hardly difficult for me to access.

Bob positioned himself behind the wheel, and we began our journey down the country roads that dominated the first portion of our journey home. Due to all the effort placed in resurrecting my vehicle, sweat had saturated my shirt and penetrated the thick fabric of my suit coat. Bob's car had been running long enough that the cooling influence of the air conditioning should have kicked in. However, there was no relief.

Reflexively, I reached for the handle with the thought of rolling down the window. Seeing the dust of the dirt road swirling around us and imagining it rapidly engulfing the cabin of the car, I suppressed this impulse. Instead, I attempted to steal a glimpse of my rescuer to sense if his body language was giving away any signs that he shared my annoyance with the heat and, more important, whether he would attempt to do something about it. My observations yielded no tension, anxiety, or motivation to act. In fact, he seemed undaunted by the searing temperature. My glimpse also allowed me to ascertain part of his secret to success.

Bob was wearing a short-sleeved shirt with a neatly pressed collar unbuttoned enough to expose grayish-brown chest hair. His pants were thin, light khaki, and a brown covered-toe sandal concealed only a fraction of his foot. I had many minutes ago conceded formality by draping my suit coat over my seat, loosening my silk tie, and unbuttoning the top two buttons of my shirt. Still, I was left with long sleeves, an undershirt unsuccessfully designed to prevent sweat from seeping into my designer shirt, heavy olive dress pants, and a pair of maroon snakeskin shoes that the salesman assured me breathed well.

Bob was smiling now. He spoke measurably, "You're wondering about my car."

I hesitated, "No, not at all."

"It's okay," he responded. "It's perfectly reasonable to question."

"Seriously, Bob, it seems like a fine car," I said, trying to cover my true thoughts.

"Let's face it, she's not much to look at. I bought it used eight years ago with cash."

"With cash?" I asked, unaccustomed to the idea that people still did such a thing.

"Yeah, it took me several years to save up. I even rode my bike or walked to work before. Of course, my job wasn't this far away at the time," he responded.

I was beginning to see the car in a whole new light.

He went on, "It has been very reliable, a good companion to me and my family. Since it is completely paid for, I don't see any sense in retiring it while it still has legs."

"That's very practical," I said sincerely while contemplating the monthly sting of my sizable car payment.

"Well, I have to admit, it doesn't seem nearly as practical on a hot summer day," he said with a laugh.

I was fascinated with an individual who clearly ran counter to the "greed is good" mantra that dominated the era. For the remaining 25 miles of our trip, Bob explained to me the unique manner in which he and his family lived their lives. We started with my top-of-mind issue: Air conditioning was neither cost effective nor environmentally friendly. It was only one of the many examples of how Bob, his wife, and two children had learned to live within their modest means. Each was content to own three sets of clothes for each season. They never borrowed money from any lending institution, nor had Bob ever applied for a credit card. Money was saved until purchases could be made with cash. Cash is how they acquired both their car and their one-story home.

"A car paid in cash is one thing, but how on earth could you afford a home?" I was genuinely puzzled.

"Early in our marriage, my wife and I lived with her parents. When our first child was born, we moved into an apartment. Slowly, we built up the capital needed to get a place of our own. I'm 46, Dr. Husain, and it has been a long road."

Bob continued to explain the extent of his commitment to this lifestyle. While believing in not borrowing from any bank or person, he also chose not to lend any money to family and friends. "Lending money does not solve the person's problem if he has to worry about eventually returning it," he reasoned.

This statement rang true as I quickly reviewed the myriad of family sessions I had overseen in which relationships were strained due to the obligations of the borrower and the expectations of the lender.

"Any cash we can consider extra, we freely give to anyone in need. We do so without any anticipation of return."

Bracing for more of his accounts, I was surprised and disheartened to find the car slowing down and coming to a stop. Throughout the conversation, we had paused intermittently for me to point him in the right direction, but I was still taken aback when we reached my house. I exited the car staggering; this seemingly average, middle aged, meager-salaried social worker had clouded my head with a litany of competing thoughts.

After this insightful experience, I made it a point to pay attention to Bob. In meetings, he would usually sit quietly and observe. On the occasions he did speak, I found his words to be wise, pragmatic, and always in the best interest of the client. His superiors mostly ignored him.

Winter was quickly approaching when Bob stopped by my office to say an unexpected goodbye. He told me he was resigning from his position. He explained to me that he was unwilling to compromise his work ethics to please a supervisor who was asking him to cut corners at a cost to the people he had sworn to help. I did not probe into the nature of his conflict but instead began to feel deep concern about his future.

"Do you have another job lined up?"

With an air of confidence, he replied, "I do not."

He thanked me for always treating him with respect. I thanked him for his kindness and, of course, the car ride home. We both hoped to run into each other in the near future.

Immediately after he left, I tried to come to grips with his decision. Had Bob thought about the implication of leaving one job before finding another? He had a family of four to support. What would he do? How could he live? Then, I smiled and realized the folly of my thinking. It was Bob who had enough money tucked away for such an occasion. It was Bob who had no car or mortgage payment that kept him up at night. It was Bob and his family who had no need for the latest fashion trend or new technology.

My anxiety for Bob was what we psychiatrists refer to as projection: I would have been incapable of making the same decision if I were put in his situation. Forced to choose between my career and my values, I would have been overwhelmed by worry stemming from bills, mortgage, car payments, and other extravagances I had accrued by not living within my considerable means. Much like that hot, summer day, Bob had left me in awe over a life that allowed him the luxury of removing himself from a situation that caused him moral and ethical discomfort. In contrast, I found myself trapped by a variety of constraints that would not have afforded me the same freedom.

In the days that followed, I began to deconstruct my own choices and why I had come to the United States in the first place. Born in Delhi, India during a time of great religious and political upheaval, my family was forced to migrate to Karachi, Pakistan when I was a young boy. In contrast to this desperate scene, the theme of my childhood could only be described by the word happiness. I was surrounded by a large and loving family. My mother instilled in me a positive self-worth, and my father promoted my every academic and athletic endeavor. As I transitioned from adolescence to adulthood, however, I became disaffected with the options that lay before me in the country of my youth. In order to access the right university, one must have a connection with the right administrator. To rise in the ranks of a profession, one must be a member of the proper political party. If you desired to start a business or secure property, a bribe to a local official might be required.

Such compromises and constraints led me to search for a society that valued a man based on his merit and effort. This voyage included stints in England and Canada before I eventually put down roots in the United States. I received training and certification in child psychiatry, obtained a professorship at the University of Missouri, published books and numerous articles in prestigious journals, and even married the first-born daughter of a Hall of Fame football coach who won Notre Dame a national title. I lived in a large home with a pool in the backyard, wore custom-made clothes, and vacationed in the locations of my choosing. By most people's standards, this man who was once a refugee, who had dark skin, spoke with an accent, and settled in central Missouri in the late 1960s had done pretty well for himself.

Somewhere on this road, however, I had diverged from my original intent. Compelled by the desire to live a life devoid of ethical compromise, I had somehow become the gatherer of possessions, titles, and things. My brief encounter with Bob taught me that I was one misstep from losing everything that I accumulated and more pressingly, that I had parted ways with control over the direction of my life. In essence, I had willingly given away a considerable portion of my power and freedom.

From that moment on, I vowed to reclaim this lost power and freedom. *Road Map to Power* is a recounting of this journey.

The first leg of this journey was embracing the insulting secret I shared with you at the beginning of this chapter: Even with the small chance I was more than average, I could never expect to dine at the table of the elite. In fact, this "secret" shouldn't be shocking at all. Most of us are average, statistically speaking. We fall under the fat, middle part of the bell curve that encompasses 68% of the population as shown in the graph below. Mathematicians call this being within plus or minus one standard deviation from the mean – the term "mean" being synonymous with "average."[1]

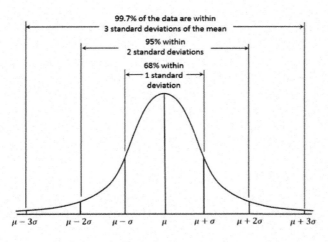

Fig. 1 Bell Curve

If you have been blessed with something a little extra or burdened by having a little less than most, then you are within plus or minus 2 standard deviations of the mean. This group, plus all the individuals considered average, make up an impressive 95% of humankind and are indicated in the same graph by adding together the before mentioned area with the smaller portions next to them. At the risk of making you dizzy or causing you to relive your worst nightmare – walking into a high school or college statistics class – let's look at one more possibility. Say you have been sprinkled with a large helping of that magical genetic fairy dust, or on the opposite end, your gene pool more likely resembles an algae filled swamp. Then we find ourselves 3 standard deviations from the mean. The three partitions at each end of the figure above is where an overwhelming 99.7% reside.

---

1   «Empirical Rule» by Dan Kernler – Own work. Licensed under CC BY-SA 4.0 via Wikimedia Commons – http://commons.wikimedia.org/wiki/File:Empirical_Rule. PNG#/media/File:Empirical_Rule.PNG.

For simplicity's sake and because it is part of our modern vernacular (chanting, "We are the 99.7%" doesn't have the same ring), I will refer to this group as the 99%.

It is extremely unlikely that you fall under the remaining 0.3% located in the gray. Too low on the bell curve and one will lack the capacity to start a book of this modest reading level. Too high on the curve and you don't need this book anyway.

While being labeled a percentile can seem dehumanizing, academics love the bell curve because it is remarkable the number of variables that fall under the normal distribution, including height, weight, and intelligence. It is as if the bell curve shape serves as integral part of Mother Nature's grand design, where differences in the human species are observable, but otherwise humans are relatively similar. If someone is extremely tall, he or she likely measures seven feet. If people are equally small, they are a hair under five feet. Take it from a guy who in his younger days used to wear shoes with a three inch sole to mask his vertical challenges. I can safely say you are going to notice if you're standing next to someone two feet taller than you.

With all the variability in this world, however, is two feet really all that much? In fact, the small range in height is one factor in how we categorize ourselves as human. If, on a mission to the deep reaches of outer space, an astronaut encountered an alien race, he or she would almost always be a fair representation for the aliens to gauge the height of our species since all known sentient life follows a normal distribution.

Of course, not all qualities follow the normal distribution pattern. This fact is especially true when human beings buck Mother Nature and artificially create a construct like money and wealth. Take the study on wealth allocation conducted by G. William Domhoff[2], professor of psychology and sociology at the University of California at Santa Cruz. According to his calculations, the richest 1% of the population in the United States owns 42% of the wealth. Stretch that out to the richest 5% and now you are accounting for 69% of the entire wealth in this country. Simple math tells us that only 31% of the nation's monetary worth is remaining for 95% of Americans to share.

Instead of a standard bell curve, wealth has been shown to follow the Pareto curve. A Pareto distribution predicts that only a few people will have a large amount of whatever is being measured, leaving a substantially smaller amount for the vast majority.

2   Domhoff GW. Wealth, Income, and Power. Updated February 2013. Retrieved October 28, 2014 from http://www2.ucsc.edu/whorulesamerica/power/wealth.html

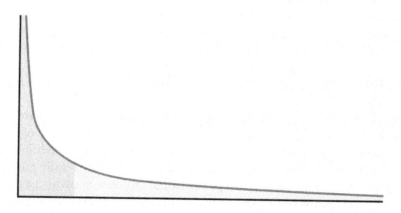

Fig. 2 Pareto Distribution

The problem with Pareto distribution is that almost everyone fails to receive an equal share of the overall pie. Before you accuse me of espousing socialist ideals, let's delve deeper into the example of height discussed earlier. In a normal distribution, like height, an average woman in the United States is about 5 feet 4 inches. A woman in the 99th percentile would be about 6 feet. The woman in the 99th percentile is about 1.125 times taller than her average counterpart. When examining wealth, however, we find an entirely different picture. To qualify for the top 50%, based on IRS statistics, your income reported on the 2011 individual or household tax return would need to be around $34,823. To qualify for the top 1%, your income reported on a 2011 tax return would need to reach a minimum level of $388,905.[3] That's about 11 times the difference. This gap becomes more staggering when the .1% is compared to the norm. To be considered a part of the .1%, an individual would have reported almost $1.6 million in income in 2011. That's about 46 times more yearly earnings than the person in the 50th percentile. Thus, an average person would need their entire working career to equal the earning power of what the .1% amasses in just one year. Imagine if height followed the same Pareto distribution as wealth: The tallest 1% of women would be standing an astonishing 59 feet and the tallest .1% at 276 feet.

Wealth, following a Pareto distribution in almost every country (some of the worst examples being socialist countries), has become the modern

---

3   McCormally K. How Do You Rank as a Taxpayer? Kiplinger, January 17, 2014. Retrieved November 13, 2014 from http://www.kiplinger.com/article/taxes/T054-C000-S001-where-do-you-rank-as-a-taxpayer.html

day barometer for power. Should it be surprising, then, that large segments of society often report feeling powerless over the forces that govern their lives or determine their success. A large source of this uneasiness is that something seems wholly unnatural about how power is distributed. I might expect to be a little taller or a little shorter than the person next to me, but 46 times taller or shorter?

What is natural is for humans to strive for mastery over the forces that affect their lives. Unfortunately, for many, mastery has been relegated to merely staying ahead of next month's bills. In our attempt to achieve power and success, we emulate the most biologically and societally endowed: politicians, corporate executives, professional athletes, showbiz personalities, and supermodels. We overextend our borrowing capacity to buy a big house, a luxury car, or a beautiful dress with the hope that it will bring the same power and prestige exhibited by the 1%. When this pursuit of wealth accompanied by material possessions fails to provide satisfaction and actually creates a scenario in which we are more powerless, we risk falling into a spiral of discontent and hopelessness. To phrase it bluntly, it isn't that people have necessarily failed to reach their potential but that their potential did not live up to some lofty standard or level that was most likely unobtainable. When you boil it down, this failure is the by-product of a mathematical miscalculation.

This conclusion demonstrates that I am not begrudging the elite their success nor devaluing it. On the contrary, my thesis centers around the idea that the level of status and accomplishment of the 1% is so remarkable, striving for power in the traditional manner is a losing proposition for all but a select few.

Therefore the first half of the book dives deeper into how the rules of power have changed to benefit only a select few, why we pursue power through strategies that will likely end in failure, and how the elite play on our beliefs of inferiority to continue their stranglehold of influence. I should warn you that some of you may experience some temporary nausea while traveling through these chapters as they call into question some of the most fundamental practices of our society. Once you have negotiated these twists and turns, however, you will find yourself in a region of the book that offers hope for the 99%. This section is dedicated to the ingredients needed to steer clear from the detours of fictitious power and the qualities paramount to arriving at a true and lasting source of empowerment.

To guide you along the way, the beginning of each chapter has a "Rule of the Road" that is designed to challenge preconceived notions associated with the pursuit, acquisition, and maintenance of power. I have also provided "Mile Markers" or key terms you will encounter throughout each chapter. "Power Points" are located at the end of each chapter to serve as a summary of the most important themes addressed. There you will also find the "Next Destination" or a quick glimpse of what to expect in the following pages.

All of these signs will point toward the direction of the final chapter: "The Road Map to Power." The road map pieces together the lessons learned throughout the book, forming the foundation for a new paradigm of personal power that is accessible and obtainable for the 99% regardless of where they fall on the normal distribution. In the drawing of the road map, you will discover that it incorporates both modern research and deep rooted principles available throughout time. If followed, it provides the traveler the chance for a life filled with self-dignity, satisfaction, and happiness.

As Bob offered me decades ago, I welcome you to join me for the ride.

Power Points

- Many biological characteristics adhere to a *bell curve* or *normal distribution* in which most people will find themselves categorized as "average."

- *Wealth,* however, follows a *Pareto distribution* in that the vast majority of assets are held by a relative few.

- Many times the pursuit of power through possessions and titles reduces choices and limits *freedom.* Sometimes, those with less to lose find themselves with the most autonomy over their life decisions.

- There exists a *road map to power* that allows for members of *the 99%* to reach a place of personal power, dignity, and happiness regardless of their location on the *normal distribution.*

Next Destination

The rules of power have changed dramatically from when our early ancestors attempted to navigate a menacing world. Now, biological endowment, inheritance, and luck are the king makers, leaving the 99% in a severe power outage.

2

A Brief History of Power

Rule of the Road: We have become more
Wal-Mart than wildebeest.

Mile Markers: Serengeti, Neanderthal, Survival, Retirement, Class Distinction, Honor Killing, Celebrity Worship, Inheritance, the Kennedys, Biological Endowment, Facebook, IQ, Cognitive Elite, Tyra Banks, Luck, Powerball, Probability

On the plains of the Serengeti, sprawling across parts of Tanzania and Kenya, a large herd of wildebeest is in the midst of a mass migration. Trailing this vast assembly is a sturdy pack of lions waiting for an opportune moment to initiate a kill. Lions possess a tremendous reputation for their hunting prowess, a distinction that is well deserved. Yet, even the most gifted of predators recognizes the futility of charging a full grown wildebeest safely secured in the heart of the herd. Instead, she waits (yes, almost always a she) for the young and the vulnerable to fall behind, wander away, or make a reckless move into the bushes where sightlines are limited. While certainly no Einstein of the animal world, it is paramount for the mother and father wildebeest to limit the mistakes of their children. One lapse of concentration, one moment of weakness, and the lions may secure the advantage they have patiently garnered. Whether it is due to a cunning foe, food shortages, inclement weather, or other factors of nature, hundreds of thousands of these migrating animals will lose their lives during this journey.

In the fluorescent illuminated rows of goods stocked 10 feet high in a Wal-Mart in Columbia, Missouri, a family of four attempts to buy groceries for the week. What seems to be a routine shopping trip is about to turn into an epic tantrum. While crossing the aisle, the couple makes the common mistake of roaming too close to the toy department. The younger of their two children keenly spots a character from his favorite TV show. Pleading to his mother and father that the purchase of this toy will complete his set, he begins an all-out assault to impose his will. Despite several emphatic repetitions of "No!" the child only intensifies his pleading. He is now in full meltdown mode, and other patrons, as well as store workers, are beginning to stare. Since Columbia is still a small enough town where people "talk," the couple succumbs to the relentless pressure of their child and places the item in their cart. Clearly rattled, the parents veer quickly to the checkout line and move hastily to their minivan in the parking lot.

In this modern age, it is difficult to believe and almost impossible to remember that human beings, for the vast majority of their extensive history, had more in common with the creatures of the Serengeti than the family of four frequenting the Wal-Mart. The way we were built and the manner in which we conducted our lives reflected an environment where we were simultaneously predator and prey. If we were to come face to face with our ancient selves, we would be looking into the eyes of a being built for strength, endurance, and agility. Our ancestor was equally adept at stalking the herd or escaping the clutches of a would-be attacker.

In the article, "Built Like a Neanderthal[4]," exercise nutritionist John M. Berardi, Ph.D., and archaeologist John K. Williams, Ph.D., teamed up to discuss the admirable, well-adapted physique of the long-ridiculed Neanderthal. Anchored in history as stooping, dim-witted oafs, Neanderthals are simply victims of an archeologist capitulating to a commonly held theory of the time. Berardi and Williams state that an 1860s French paleontologist, eager to provide an ape-like ancestor to the millions indoctrinated by Charles Darwin's newly-released On the Origin of Species, offered the crippled bones of an elderly Neanderthal man as the norm for the species. The reality of Neanderthal man was starkly different, for he was "the big-

4   Berardi JM, Williams JK. Built Like a Neanderthal, Part I. August 8, 2005. Retrieved October 28, 2014 from http://www.t-nation.com/free_online_article/sports_body_training_performance_science/built_like_a_neanderthal_1

die because of self-inflicted causes such as poor diet, stressful life choices, and reckless behavior then anything Mother Nature can throw at you.

This rapid advancement and the ability of human beings to increasingly conquer the elements has also had its negative consequence. For instance, greater societal complexity led to the rise of an additional phenomenon that would penetrate the fabric of every culture: class distinction. The external placement of value on groups of people based on the societal functions they performed was the beginning of class distinction. Functions that were valued poorly resulted in people who were valued poorly. Functions that were valued highly resulted in people who were valued highly. The class system, and all of its ascription bias and deprivation of power, became firmly entrenched. Class isolated its members, making the potential vocations, spouses, and earning potential of those within the class virtually prescribed for them. This affected the lower classes of people in a devastating manner, condemning people with devalued status to limited resources and prospects.

Even in today's enlightened age, for those who dare hope for or act against the established class boundaries, traumatic resistance and menacing, even deadly consequences abound. Consider the tragic romance of the now-infamous Jassi and Mithu, whose story illustrates the enduring constraints of India's caste system and the coercive power that—visibly and invisibly—pervades class distinctions around the world. Their story has commanded worldwide attention. It was profiled in the United States on investigative journalism programs such as Dateline and 20/20, featured in the Canadian made-for-television movie Murder Unveiled, and archived online in tributes, petitions, news articles, and Mithu's own Justice for Jassi website.

Jassi was a single, affluent, well-educated young Indian woman who lived with her family, according to Sikh tradition for unwed daughters, in Vancouver, Canada. In 1994, on a visit to India with her parents, she met and fell in love with Mithu, a rickshaw driver. Jassi communicated with him secretly for four years before returning on another family trip to India. Taking advantage of the opportunity, and unbeknownst to her family, Jassi and Mithu were married. Returning home with her relatives, this young bride lived apart from her low-caste spouse for two years — a period in which her relatives eventually discovered her marriage and subsequently beat her, confined her, bribed her, and orchestrated a plot to falsely accuse her beloved.

When she finally escaped in 2000, Jassi borrowed cash from a friend and went to India to be with Mithu. But their happiness would be short-lived. After less than one month together as husband and wife, Jassi and Mithu were ambushed on their way home from the market. Thrown from their motorcycle in a sword attack, Mithu was beaten and left for dead, while Jassi was kidnapped and taken to an abandoned farmhouse. Phone records indicate that her mother and uncle were on the phone with her killers only minutes before her brutal murder. Her mother allegedly gave the order for the kidnappers to slit her daughter's throat in what is known as an "honor killing," one of the most perverse ways of ensuring that people restrict themselves to what is socially acceptable for their class.

Admittedly, this story serves as an extreme example of the rigidity of class distinction. More regularly, people marry outside of their culture, religion, ethnicity, and class. Jassi and Mithu's deaths, however, illustrate an important evolution in power dynamics. As we move further away from the realities of ancestors, power—how it is defined, what it looks like, and how it is obtained and maintained—fundamentally changes. A world where food, often scarce, was either hunted or gathered cannot be compared to a world where people drive a mile down a road and have dozens of choices to obtain a precooked meal. A world where strength and agility were the prerequisite for survival and the survival of one's family cannot be compared to a world where these same characteristics are most valuable in arenas of recreation like football, basketball, and soccer. Understanding this evolution lessens the surprise that modern-day visions of power are dominated by celebrity, cash, and opulent living and are often accompanied by personal attendants, huge fan bases, and paparazzi. We are, after all, more Wal-Mart than wildebeest.[7]

As a people, we have drifted away from a power base that was rooted in the physique and brain power of mankind to a society in which the embodiment of power lies in the single individual and his personal status—earned or ascribed to him—as a member of the elite. The elite possess the resources necessary for distinguishing themselves from the masses and thereby catapulting themselves to the center of public interest and esteem. People with such affluence operate with apparently few restrictions in life. They enjoy frequent fine dining; lavish vacations; expensive homes, cars,

---

7   The Bedouins of the Arabian Peninsula referred to their leader as Shaykh and considered him "the first among equals." This carefully crafted title was an acknowledgment of the importance of putting no individual above another as each member of the tribe was essential in dealing with the challenges of a nomadic existence.

and wardrobes; private education; domestic help; and entry into exclusive social networks. As an emotional bonus, they gain respect merely for their financial ability to participate in elite activities and for the beauty and rareness of their possessions. If they infringe upon the laws of the land, the privileged can call upon an army of lawyers and representatives to reduce or, in some societies, simply eliminate penalties.

The media age has allowed the elite and all their abundances to be revered and even worshipped by the masses. What started in 1984 as a way of "sharing champagne and caviar dreams" by the Lifestyles of the Rich and Famous has exploded into a host of shows celebrating the glamorous life. Over the years, shows such as MTV Cribs, Keeping Up with the Kardashians, HGTV's Million Dollar Rooms (not houses), and The Real Housewives of ... (insert city), whet our appetite for a lifestyle that most people can only access in their wildest fantasies. Thus, the materially enriched find themselves well provided for and socially revered, a powerful combination to be sure.

Despite the variance displayed among the coveted lifestyles of the rich and famous, the elite draw their power from common sources: inheritance and material wealth, biological endowments, and good, old-fashioned luck. Thus, if you are looking to be powerful in the way that modern society has defined power, these three avenues are far and away the most likely paths to achieving this goal. Taking a moment to examine each of these pathways highlights the dilemma for the bell curve's 99% and their pursuit of a slice of the power pie.

Inheritance is perhaps the most firmly established source of power. It passes the assets of a predecessor on to his heirs. In this fashion, property, status, wealth, and even ruling power have remained in families for generations. The most well-known archetype of inheritance is the one we associate with monarchies, in which the powerful privileges awarded to kings and queens are available exclusively to their bloodline heirs.

Haji Hassanal Bolkiah, sultan of Brunei, is the latest in a long line of his forebears to benefit from a dynasty that stretches back over 600 years. A 2008 article from the website Hottnez features some of the world's richest monarchs and their residences. Sultan Bolkiah stands out from even the most extravagantly rich with his collection of cars, numbering between 3,000 and 6,000, and a palace considered the largest in the world at over two million square feet. That's about the size of 40 White Houses stacked on top of each other. The enormity of the Sultan's possessions reflects the "spare no expense" lifestyle that seems to envelop royalty. Compared to most people of the world, whose workaday living often provides less than enough to supply their basic needs, the most appealing feature of royalty may be the notion of being "set for life" without a worry or care about financial security or material provisions.

Inheritance is not only for those with royal blood, as we know from witnessing the histories of business dynasties and political legacies. The Rockefellers, Trumps, and Kennedys all represent families who passed on great wealth, privilege, celebrity, and influence to future generations. The Kennedy family, perhaps best known for the mass appeal of former U.S. President John F. Kennedy, is one whose valor, tragedy, scandal, achievements, and glamour have been broadcast worldwide for more than half a century. In a February 2010 blog post, former Congressional correspondent, Time Magazine writer, and national political correspondent for The Washington Post Karen Tumulty notes that "next January [2011] will mark the first time in 64 years that there has not been a Kennedy in [U.S.] federal office." Tumulty's comment reflects the 2010 departure of Patrick Kennedy, son of Senator Edward Kennedy, from Congress. After she wrote this, Joseph P. Kennedy III was elected to the U.S. Congress in November 2012, making the absence from elected office for the first family of politics a scant 10 months.

Younger Kennedys inherited the political legacy of their grandfather, Joseph P. Kennedy, Sr., a Harvard-educated man of political ambition. Joe Kennedy raised his children for success, determined that their Irish Catholic heritage would not deny them any opportunity or esteem. He became their example—a successful stock market investor, the first chairman of the Securities Exchange Commission, and a U.S. ambassador to Britain. Eventually, three of his four sons would go on to hold the high offices of Attorney General, Senator, and President. Two of his five daughters also made significant contributions at home and abroad, with one founding the Special Olympics and the other serving as U.S. Ambassador to Ireland. Partly due to their own guile but certainly boosted by the power these children inherited from their well-connected, ambitious father, the Kennedy family has enjoyed political influence that shapes the United States even today.

For those who inherit the status of their parents it seems no time is wasted. From kings to politicians to entrepreneurs, the grooming to wield power begins in childhood. Incubated by wealth and privilege, the elite receive private tutoring, matriculate at prestigious schools, and are promoted to positions of great responsibility at young ages.

You, on the other hand, most likely attended public schools, worked your first job at or near minimum wage, and became heir to the old family car. While fairy tales tout true love as the way for young maidens and poor farm boys to breach the royal moat and partake of royal treasures and acclaim, reality forces us to pause our Disney movies and admit that such encounters are far from likely in our lives. Truly, the inherited power of royalty is unavailable to the masses. Such exclusion is obvious from birth. We are relegated to nicknaming our daughters "princess" and buying royal costumes from a litany of department stores to fill their trunks full of dress-up clothes. It is probably safe to say that, in your quest for power, you can cross inheriting a fortune off the list.

If inheritance is not in the cards, then those next in line to reap the rewards of this earth possess yet another source of power: biological assets of extraordinary physical ability, intelligence, or beauty. This form of power is most rooted in human beings' ancestral nature. As mentioned earlier in the chapter, since a large portion of the population is no longer locked in a day to day battle for survival, these biological talents are displayed in new and more elaborate venues. Today, cultures place increasingly excessive value on individual biological accomplishment on the public stage: the football player breaking a tackle and stiff-arming his way to a touchdown, a classical pianist enrapturing the crowd during a performance at Carnegie Hall, and an actor baring his rock-solid abs and showcasing his stunning looks on a giant movie screen. In such an environment, the people who are born with exceptional biological assets garner attention and praise and are fast-tracked into a world of privilege bent on developing and exploiting their unusual gifts. These people are chosen to perform highly valued functions in society and consequently merit more influence, more esteem, and more compensation.

China, a country of 1.3 billion people, saw a lone 22-year-old, perhaps its most famous nonpolitical figure yet, achieve worldwide celebrity in 2002. That was when Yao Ming, a 7'6" Chinese Basketball Association Most Valuable Player and Olympic athlete, signed a contract with the U.S. National Basketball Association's Houston Rockets. Yao's formal basketball training began at age nine and he was playing for the China National Team (CNT) by age 18. All this youthful accomplishment is profiled on the NBA's official website, which mentions that his 6'3" mother also enjoyed a CNT stint. Not to be outdone, his father, who stands at a not too shabby 6'7", also played basketball professionally. After furious negotiations that would make Henry Kissinger proud, Yao was drafted by the NBA's Houston Rockets on the first pick in the 2002 draft. Three years later, Yao parlayed his exceptional ability into a 5-year, $75 million contract. Despite a career slowed by various injuries that ultimately forced an early retirement, Yao averaged 19.1 points and 9.3 rebounds, led the Rockets to four playoff appearances, and was named an All-Star five times.

A man born with great potential for height and athletic prowess, Yao represents the upward mobility associated with early-encouraged endowments. A 2004 BusinessWeek article[8] covering Yao's Chinese endorsement deals reminds us of "athletes who by dint of raw talent, force of will, and power of personality transcend national borders and become mythical figures to people all over the planet." Biological endowments don't stop at awarding bearers the obvious benefits of their exceptional traits. They enjoy exceptional admiration and acclaim as well.

Few have enjoyed the level of "out of nowhere" acclaim like Mark Zuckerberg. Ben Menzrich's book, Accidental Billionaires, and the Academy Award winning movie it inspired, The Social Network, chronicle the meteoric rise of the Facebook co-founder. What started as an ambitious idea turned into a global phenomenon that touts over 1.39 billion participants. Facebook has been credited for keeping friends and families spread across the world close, fanning the flames of love, fueling social and political revolutions, posing as an international security threat, and serving as the bane of many a company and organization as countless work hours from employees are lost while they "update their status." Regardless of the differing perspectives, Facebook is a massive success. While stock valuations vary, CNN Money has estimated the company's value at $200 billion and growing. As the primary shareholder, Zuckerberg makes Forbes' list of the 400 wealthiest Americans, currently no. 16 with a net worth of $33.3 billion. At this writing, Facebook is trading for around $74 per share. In one day of trading, Zuckerberg netted nearly a billion dollars. And the sale was considered a mild disappointment.

The book title, Accidental Billionaire, (though not necessarily the contents of the book) gives the impression that Zuckerberg and people like him wandered into this extreme wealth and subsequent fame. It almost makes one feel like the average Joe or Jane could follow the same path and slip into superstardom. Yet, a close investigation of Zuckerberg's life shows

---

8   Lowry T, Roberts D. Wow! Yao! Bloomberg Businessweek Magazine, October 24, 2004. Retrieved October 28, 2014 from http://www.businessweek.com/stories/2004-10-24/wow-yao

that he has always been far from ordinary. The Harvard Crimson[9] states that Zuckerberg was already well into computer programming in his early teens. His superior intellect allowed him access to prestigious secondary schools such as Phillips Exeter. In high school he created an MP3 application that was featured in PC Magazine. He even earned a perfect score of 1600 on his SATs.

Throughout his life, Zuckerberg has exhibited a clear genetic endowment that has propelled him to the upper stratosphere of recognition and status. The same can be said of other tycoons of the technological age such as Bill Gates and Steve Jobs. While none inherited a kingdom, they were given the gift of superior intelligence that, when applied properly, would allow them to dominate a generation. Intelligence is called upon for some of the most basic functions of human survival—learning, applying knowledge and solving problems—and has far-reaching effects on a person's experiences throughout life. It is also one that many cultures spend years developing, believing that it is the most reliable way to better oneself and ensure positive outcomes for one's future. But the intellectual grooming received by the masses is limited in its outcomes by the genetic lottery clearly won by the likes of Zuckerberg, Gates, and Jobs.

To illustrate my point more clearly, let's examine a concept with which most individuals have a working familiarity: the intelligence quotient. Modern IQ tests use a variety of methods to test multiple areas of intelligence. Psychologists Alfred Binet, Theodore Simon, and William Stern first researched and developed this idea. IQ tests are measured using percentiles, which show how a person's score measures against the scores of the rest of the population. IQ scores of the U.S. population fall almost perfectly into the bell curve pattern discussed in Chapter 1. This normal distribution shows that 68% of people score within a range of 85 to 115 and have what researchers call "average intelligence." The remainder of the bell curve distribution houses the minority of people, split evenly among two extremes: low intelligence and above-average intelligence. Those attempting to improve their IQ standing run into the barrier that this metric is remarkably consistent throughout their lifetime, leaving them at the mercy of their initial biology.

---

9   Grynbaum MM. Mark E. Zuckerberg '06: The whiz behind thefacebook.com. *The Harvard Crimson*, June 10, 2004. Retrieved October 28, 2014 from http://www. thecrimson.com/article/2004/6/10/mark-e-zuckerberg-06-the-whiz/

In 1994, Richard Herrnstein and Charles Murray published a book, *The Bell Curve*[10], designed to explain the variations in intelligence among Americans. Although their conclusions and indeed the very evidence of intellectual variance are highly controversial, Herrnstein and Murray's work brought much attention to the fact that only a small percentage of the population has the intellectual ability to seize the many opportunities available in American society. Members of what Herrnstein and Murray call a "cognitive elite" are able to use their higher intelligence to make more money and send their children to better schools. Those in this group are able to easily secure positions of great advantage. They are able to advance educationally, politically, socially, and financially because of their exceptional intelligence. It is this group that sets the agenda for the remainder of society in fields such as law, industry, politics, and education.

While IQ is the most documented tool for measuring a person's intelligence, specialists from many fields have sought alternative means to explain and quantify this trait. Communications instructor Julie Yingling has written on the idea of tabula rasa, or blank slate, in her book *A Lifetime of Communication*.[11] Tabula rasa is the idea that infants are born with no innateness and that everything they learn is a result of the environment into which they are born. This idea seems to offer more hope than IQ since it renders infants equally blank-minded as opposed to endowed with a fixed intellectual capability or innate body of knowledge. But a person has no more control over his birth environment than he has over his genetics, and birth environments vary immensely. The implication of all these theories is clear: whether it is the intelligence quotient or tabula rasa, intelligence is derived from factors we cannot choose, control, or improve.

Physical superiority and intelligence are not the only biological features that remain fixtures in society and propel individuals into superstardom. Gordon L. Patzer, Ph.D., then dean of the College of Business Administration at Roosevelt University, was interviewed in a 2004 Dateline NBC episode that asked if a person's appearance really mattered. "A person's physical attractiveness—the look that she/he is basically born with—impacts every individual literally from birth until death," he said. "People are valued more who are higher in physical attractiveness. As distasteful as that might be, that's the reality." And Patzer would know. He's spent 30 years research-

---

10 Herrnstein RJ, Murray C. *The Bell Curve: Intelligence and Class Structure in American Life*. New York: Free Press Paperbacks, 1996. Available at http://www.amazon.com/Bell-Curve-Intelligence-Structure-Paperbacks/dp/0684824299

11 Yingling J. *A Lifetime of Communication: Transformations through Relational Dialogues*. Hove, East Sussex, UK: Psychology Press, 2004.

ing, writing, and speaking about the Physical Attractiveness Phenomenon, which holds that the "assumptions, expectations, attitudes, and behaviors" triggered by a person's physical attractiveness cause "pervasive, powerful effects," limiting those who lack allure while benefiting beauties, according to Patzer's website (http://gordonpatzer.com/).

Attractiveness has the added importance of allowing for two pathways to achieving power. Attractive people may broker their looks into marriage with mates of great status, in essence, a variation of inherited power. Or this trait can stand alone and hold value on its own merit. Supermodels such as Tara Banks and Heidi Klum have cashed in on their faces and figures, drawing yearly incomes in the millions and iconic status internationally. According to the U.S. Bureau of Labor Statistics, job qualifications for models include "flawless skin, healthy hair, and attractive facial features."[12] Given the abundance of ads peddling products to help consumers achieve just that, it is more than painfully obvious that not all Americans stand an equal chance of becoming successful models.

Before you become too discouraged by looking in the mirror and realizing that despite modern advancements in skin cream, you are no supermodel, realize that there still remains one last hope for power and prestige. You could always be lucky. Take, for instance, the inspiring true story of the Minnesota school lunch ladies. These 16 inspirational women went about their lives in relative obscurity in the small town of Holdingford, which boasts a population of under 1,000. Pooling their modest resources (most were earning a wage of under $10 an hour), they were frequent players of the nationwide lottery contest known as Powerball. In 2003, their gamble paid off as they were the proud recipients of 50% of a $191 million Powerball jackpot. While phenomenal it its own right, what endeared these humble women to the American public was their unlikely reaction to winning such a sum. According to the Roger Carlson, Superintendent of Holdingford Schools, 12 of the 16 women remained employed with the district despite their stroke of fortune.

Spend an hour perusing the Powerball official website and you will find several stories of regular people becoming instant multi-millionaires. It is an ingenious marketing strategy aimed at the majority of Americans eager for a lifetime of comfort. As lottery players' line of thinking goes, "If these people were able to do it, why not me?" While it might be difficult to relate to Tiger Woods or Prince Charles, walking a mile in the shoes of Christo-

12   Bureau of Labor Statistics. Demonstrators, Product Promoters, and Models.
      Retrieved October 28, 2014 from http://www.careerfitter.com/reports/2000reports/
      az/ocos253.htm

pher Shaw of Marshall, Missouri may not be such a leap. The Powerball website states that Chris, the winner of a $258.5 million jackpot, worked at a gas station convenience store and as a truck driver.

Click on a different link, however, and one will find the odds of winning this Grand Prize: a mind boggling 1 in 195,249,054. Even the odds of winning a $100 prize are 1 in 13,644. To put this number in perspective, you could buy a thousand tickets every day for 100 years and still only have around a 5% chance of taking home the grand prize.

The concept of luck in determining success goes beyond simply picking the right six numbers. In many cases, the biologically talented require good fortune equivalent to winning the lottery in order to obtain celebrity status. Take the case of British singing sensation Susan Boyle. At first glance, Ms. Boyle is as dreary as the prototypical English weather. In fact, she was openly mocked in her initial appearance on Britain's Got Talent, a show that would garner her worldwide recognition. Despite Susan's plain looks and folksy demeanor, she possessed a voice that would earn her the role of soloist in the choir of angels. By singing with bravado Broadway standards such as "I Dreamed a Dream" from Les Miserables and "Memory" from Cats, Boyle endeared herself to the masses. Suddenly her lack of beauty and perceived naiveté fit nicely into a storyline of a simple person with one extraordinary gift. Such was her appeal, Susan's debut album sold over three million copies.

Imagine the forces of nature that must have lined up in order for this real-life fairytale to come true. First, you obviously must have some natural singing prowess. Still, walk into any random bar during karaoke night and you will find two or three singers who mesmerize the crowd (coincidentally, Boyle was one of these karaoke stars before she became famous). Secondly, you would require an individual in your life who recognized your talent and helped cultivate it. For Susan, it was her singing coach, Fred O'Neil. Next, you would need a forum to showcase your talents: Susan had the good fortune to be alive during a time in human history where all forms of media were obsessed with the desire to find the next big thing. Last, there must exist mediums that spread the performance across continents into multiple countries, cities, and towns. Facebook, Twitter, and YouTube took what would have been a relatively local occurrence into a global phenomenon.

I hope that by now, you are coming to an important realization: As a member of the 99%, you are unlikely to have the inheritance, biological endowment, or the lightning-in-the-bottle luck it takes to be powerful by the contemporary standards by which power is defined. Still, we remain focused on the few who possess such qualities, as though they hold the key for how we, too, might unlock the door to a powerful existence ... the hope that someday, we too will have unlimited access to the status symbols of the finest homes and cars, and expensive vacations and attire.

To illustrate this concept further, let's take you back to where this chapter started. You are a member of a family of wildebeests, and you are told that on the other side of the rugged plain of the Serengeti is an oasis filled with all the luxuries and comforts a wildebeest could desire. You are also informed, however, that only 3 out of the 1,000 of your kind will actually reach this paradise. Any opportunity has the element of risk, but this venture has become a fool's quest. For the vast numbers of the herd, the oasis has become a mirage. Before they can turn back, almost all will be consumed by predators, die of dehydration or starvation, or forced to stop and settle for whatever leftovers the desert has to offer. Knowing these likely scenarios, would you even consider embarking on this journey?

For some of you, nature metaphors might not be the most compelling tool to drive home my point. How about a more modern example: would you walk into a casino and play a million-dollar slot machine that you only had a 0.3% chance of winning? Maybe, if it only cost you a quarter or a few bills in your pocket. What if, instead, you were asked to stake your life? I trust you would say "no" and walk swiftly to the nearest exit. Amazingly, many of us take on these odds with the expectancy of success. And what is even more amazing is that to do otherwise would require tremendous strength and restraint.

In our attempt to achieve power and success, we emulate the most biologically and societally endowed: the politicians, corporate executives, professional athletes, showbiz personalities, and supermodels. We overextend our borrowing capacity to buy a big house, a luxury car, or a beautiful dress with the hope that it will bring the same power and the prestige exhibited by the 1%. And when this pursuit of wealth accompanied by material possessions fails to provide satisfaction and actually creates a scenario in which we are more powerless, we risk falling into a spiral of discontent and hopelessness. Thus, we are left with a choice: play the familiar game that is clearly rigged with the fleeting hope of defying the considerable odds for disappointment, or find an alternative road to power, the one less traveled, that allows all seekers to reach their destination regardless of preconditions and variables outside their control.

Power Points

- Early human beings were built to withstand the harsh conditions of their environment, and power was distributed fairly evenly as each individual was essential to the *survival* of the group.

- As humans better adapted to their environment, the nomadic life gave way to settlements, power became more centralized in those consider most valuable, and *class distinction* emerged.

- Those attempting to elevate beyond their *class distinction* were often met with strident opposition and severe ramifications.

- Today, power is most readily obtained through **inheritance**, **biological endowment**, and **luck**. Some require a combination of these foundations of power to climb to the heights of the most distinguished classes.

- All three avenues to traditional power are mostly blocked to the members of the 99%. Yet, individuals continue to pursue power and wealth through these sources even though the *probability* for success is designed to be less than 1%.

Next Destination

Unrealistic expectations and the illusion of equality are unintended consequences when myth becomes blended with reality to form the fabric of a nation.

3

The Legend of Equality

Rule of the Road: When you get to the part about "created equal," keep reading.

"We hold these truths to be self-evident, that all men are created equal."
—Declaration of Independence, July 4th, 1776

Mile Markers: Paul Bunyan; Babe the Blue Ox; Folklore; Founding Fathers; Joe Mauer; Quick Swing; Minnesota Twins; Redemption; Little League; Fundamental Attribution Error; Individualism; Thomas Jefferson; Declaration of Independence; Life, Liberty, and the Pursuit of Happiness

Travel due north up U.S. Highway 169 from the Twin Cities, trace the entire eastern boundary of Lake Mille Lacs, execute a 90-degree left turn on to State Highway 18, and you will find yourself in the Minnesota town of Brainerd. While best known to the rest of country for its depiction in the film Fargo, most Minnesotans remember this Mississippi River destination as the home of a true statewide icon. Thousands of boys and girls, accompanied by their mothers and fathers, have made the pilgrimage to Brainerd to see the 26-foot-tall Paul Bunyan statue looming large off the outskirts of the city. Those willing to make the journey were rewarded with the seemingly miraculous sight of this giant man speaking, in his booming voice, the names and hometowns of every child who walked by.

This statue celebrates the mythological man whose larger-than-life exploits literally helped shape the landscape of Minnesota. According to American lore, Paul Bunyan was delivered to his parents' doorstep in Bangor, Maine by five giant storks. Instead of sleeping in a crib, which he easily crushed, Paul was rocked in a wagon. A farmer's entire herd of cows was designated to provide the milk he needed on a daily basis. In a short time, Paul grew so large that his very movements became destructive. By rolling over, he destroyed several acres of forest; by jumping into a body of water, he started a tidal wave. Faced with such a grand predicament, the Bunyans moved to the more spacious, less settled territory of Minnesota.

As Paul grew into a man, Minnesota became his playground. While on one of his numerous adventures, Paul discovered a baby ox notable for his giant size and a skin frozen blue by a particularly harsh winter. From that day forward, Babe the Blue Ox would become Paul's constant companion and notorious sidekick.

In legend, Paul and Babe's physical impact on the North Country was considerable. With a mighty swing of his axe, he cleared areas of forest large enough to produce enough timber for a new settlement. To ensure the speedy delivery of this timber, Paul grasped the end of a trail with his mighty hands and pulled out all of its curves. Trekking through the winter wonderland, Paul's and Babe's footsteps created large craters in the earth. When the snow melted in the spring, these craters filled with water, shaping the over 10,000 lakes scattered throughout the state.[13] On these same walks, Paul dragged his substantial axe behind him, leaving a long, winding trench. This path would become the mighty Mississippi River.

Despite all they were credited with accomplishing, like many heroes, Paul and Babe became the victims of rapidly changing times and advancing technology. Machines were furnished that were able to best the strength

---

13   A quick sidebar regarding Minnesota's lakes: I remember flying over Minnesota for the first time and being impressed by the myriad bodies of water. I thought, "Wow, maybe calling it the land of 10,000 lakes is no exaggeration." When I found out the state motto was actually an underestimation and that the total was closer to 15,000, I was shocked. I was dumbfounded, a few years later, when I discovered that Wisconsin actually has more lakes than Minnesota. Just don't rub this in the face of any Minnesotan; they are still reeling from the whole Brett Favre experiment and the memory of the Packers Super Bowl title is still fresh.

and speed of the man and his ox. Even the Brainerd statue commemorating the great mythical man was almost wiped from the history books. The talking Paul came under threat from what has come to symbolize the progress and expanse of capitalism: the mega-department store. While demolition was certainly an undignified fate, for many locals, the alternative could hardly be considered a more desirable outcome: South Dakota offered to take Paul off of Minnesota's hands. Thankfully (from the Minnesota perspective), Dick Rademacher decided the statue of Paul was just the thing to draw more guests to a nearby tourist attraction known as This Old Farm. Today, young and old can ride a roller coaster or the Tilt-a-Whirl, take a tour of a ghost mine, drift into the sky on a Ferris wheel, eat a hotdog, wash it down with some pop, and say hello to Mr. Paul Bunyan.

Though even the shadows of Paul and Babe have faded away, their emotional and social significance in many communities of Minnesota remains strong. In fact, the mere mention of Brainerd first in our discussion of Paul and Babe is probably considered a slight to some of the 14,000 citizens of Bemidji, Minnesota. These residents could raise the argument that Bemidji, not Brainerd, first devised the idea to build a monument to this Minnesota legend. In 1937, 12 years before his first sighting in Brainerd, an 18-foot-tall Paul Bunyan statue was constructed in Bemidji. An equally tall shotgun was created and set next to the big man either to symbolize his tremendous power or to appease the duck and deer hunters that frequented the area.

Bemidji had been struck by such an intense case of Bunyan fever, one website promoting the town goes so far as to claim that Bemidji was actually Paul's birthplace. So, naturally, the residents couldn't stop at just a Bunyan statue. Two years later, Paul's sidekick was meshed together out of wood, steel, and cement. Babe was fashioned in a manner that allowed him to be mobile. Aided by a truck that could fit in his underbelly, the Blue Ox was a fixture at numerous parades and festivals. Now, both Paul and Babe, a little older and worse for the wear, can be found enjoying their retirement on the banks of Lake Bemidji. Maybe they are scouting for walleye or simply relaxing as they watch the beauty of each passing sunset.

As if two giant statues of Mr. Bunyan weren't enough, the people of Akeley, Minnesota would like to submit their 25-foot-tall statue of Paul for your consideration. Please also note that their Paul is down on one knee; just imagine how tall he would be if he were standing at full salute. Built in 1949, this Bunyan is distinct for the large axe on which he rests his massive body and an enormous outstretched hand close to ground level. Although

Paul may not be able to hold the whole world in his hands, he at least can clutch you long enough for a friend or family member to take a photo.

Bunyan tributes are not just limited to rugged Minnesotans. Statues and artifacts of this mighty man can be found in at least 19 states including Arizona, California, Colorado, Florida, Idaho, Illinois, Indiana, Maine, Michigan, Missouri, New Jersey, New Mexico, New York, North Dakota, Ohio, Oklahoma, Oregon, Washington, and Wisconsin.

What drives such a strong, countrywide fascination? Consider the definition of folklore as provided by the United Nations Educational, Scientific and Cultural Organization: "Folklore (or traditional and popular culture) is the totality of tradition-based creations of a cultural community, expressed by a group or individuals and recognized as reflecting the expectations of a community insofar as they reflect its cultural and social identity." If Paul Bunyan is the reflection of the "expectations of a community," then it demonstrates some potent notions of said community. Paul Bunyan represents a group of people who desire control over the environmental forces surrounding them. It is humankind and the human spirit that will shape nature, not vice versa. Not only will the strongest and fittest of us survive and thrive, they will be chronicled in our tales passed on from generation to generation. Paul Bunyan is power embodied by physical strength and size. However, if his statues are any indication of his imagined stature, he still needs to grow some more before he could challenge the 1% on the Pareto height distribution discussed in Chapter 1.

A certain irony exists: While the founding fathers were promoting the revolutionary idea of "all men are created equal," it is greatness that is constantly being sought out and emulated. And greatness is actually a form of inequality in that it distinguishes an individual as being more than an equal to his or her counterparts. Could this idea be an affront or a contradiction to the most enduring words of the Declaration of Independence? Before we jump to such lofty conclusions, it is important to realize that Paul Bunyan's impact on the population has limitations. No adult aspires to be Paul Bunyan. No child goes to bed at night and dreams of becoming this man, just as no child believes they will grow up to be the next Santa Claus or Easter Bunny. Thus, legend and folklore have a specific niche in the role of establishing the identity of a culture and society. They provide explanations for phenomena of the world that can only be described as miraculous. They allow for people young and old to expand their imaginations and contemplate the impossible. Yet, at the end of the day, these stories are intangible and relegated to the realm of fantasy. These characters of legend cannot be touched, heard, or felt by a modern audience. Their exploits cannot be witnessed. The wonderment of youth is inevitably replaced by the skepticism of adulthood.

So, what happens when in our lifetime earthly beings perform acts of seemingly superhuman brilliance for the entire world to see? What impact might these individuals have in challenging our conceptions of equality?

Such a man was born on April 13, 1983 in the firmly middle class St. Paul neighborhood of Highland Park. Years earlier, Minnesota Twins World Series hero Jack Morris and Hall of Famer Dave Winfield called this same area home. Not quite like being born on Krypton but not too shabby of a baseball pedigree. Parents Jake Jr. and Theresa hadn't even had a chance to potty train him when they realized Joseph Patrick Mauer was a special child. An early VHS video shows him honing that electric swing that would ultimately lead to three American League batting titles. He was two years old.

The youngest of three boys, Joe had to develop his skills fast in order to keep up with the talents of his older brothers, Jake III and Billy. At the age of four, Joe was forced to quit T-ball for fear of injuring the other children with his big swing. From that moment on, Joe would be playing with kids three to four years his senior. When he was seven, he was relegated to chasing after balls hit by his brothers and their friends, but by the time he was eight, he was routinely one of the best players. Joe, Jake, and Billy were extremely competitive with one another and could turn even a game of wastebasket paper toss into a life or death event. Not surprisingly, Joe wasn't satisfied at excelling at one single game. He had to become a master at whatever sport or athletic endeavor he attempted.

While Joe didn't have a big blue ox to follow him around, he possessed a legendary contraption that was his constant companion while growing up. It was called the Quick Swing, a diabolical mechanism built by his father. Most pitching machines or swing aids use regular baseballs and full size bats. This method proved too easy for Joe. Thus, Dad replaced the baseballs with little whiffle balls used for practicing golf and the bat with a one-inch diameter pipe. While mere mortals like you and I would struggle to hit one ball from this machine, it was reported that Joe could handily hit 50 times in a row.

Such a protégé needs the appropriate venue to showcase his skills. The gods and goddesses had Mount Olympus; Joe Mauer had Cretin-Derham Hall. Most schools would be satisfied with one great athlete, but CDH is such a bastion of sports success that they boast a starting lineup of professional stars: Chris Wienke (Heisman trophy winner and former NFL quarterback), Paul Molitor (member of the 3000 hit club, World Series MVP, and 1st ballot Hall of Famer), Steve Walsh (University of Miami standout and #1 NFL draft pick); Matt Birk (6-time pro bowl center); and Michael Floyd (former Notre Dame star wide receiver and 1st round draft pick). The list continues, but I think you get the point.

Not content to shine in a single sport, Joe was the heart and soul of CDH's football, basketball, and baseball teams. During his tenure, these teams with such a rich sports history experienced unparalleled success. In basketball, Joe was the leading scorer for a team that made it to the state semifinals. He was named All State in basketball in both his 11th and 12th grade year. As the starting quarterback, Joe led his team to a state championship his junior year and a runner-up finish his senior year. In baseball, he was the starting catcher for the baseball team that captured the state title. Mauer was such a gifted and multi-talented athlete, he was named USA Today's high school player of the year in both football and baseball. These awards in football and baseball, given out annually since 1981, had never been given to the same person before nor have they since. In fact, not being a Minnesota native myself, this honor served as my first exposure to Joe Mauer. I can still picture the creative photo plastered on the front page of the sports section with Mauer seemingly split symmetrically in half. One side showed Mauer in his football attire, complete with helmet and pads. The other side depicted Mauer in his baseball garb, adorned in his jersey and cap.

While he was heavily courted by multiple colleges as a football player, it was baseball in which Joe proved he was truly transcendent. Throughout his high school career, he was a .567 hitter. His senior year, he decided to up the average to .605. During the state championship semifinals, played as a doubleheader, Joe was situated at his normal catcher position. In the second game, he caught the first five frames before being inserted as the pitcher for five more and earning an extra-inning win. Yet, he wasn't just a local wonder kid. Joe was chosen for the U.S. Youth National Team for which he was the starting catcher three years running. His natural ability proved to be worthy of the global stage as he was named the top hitter of the 2000 world championship.

What Joe didn't do, however, is what truly personified his high school career. In his four years of high school baseball, Joe never struck out. Well, except for that one time. The one instance Joe Mauer failed to make contact with the ball or earn a walk earned the most dramatic response from the dugout. They all believed some tragedy had befallen their teammate. The scene must have been reminiscent of that afternoon in Mudville when the Mighty Casey was up to bat.

By the time Mauer graduated high school, his on-the-field accomplishments were in the collective consciousness of the proverbial sports fans. Still, many communities can lay claim to a superstar whose gifts carry beyond the local American Legion baseball diamond. For Joe to enter a higher stratosphere, to enter the realm of legend, he needed a storyline that is woven in the fabric of Americana.

Here is where Jake Sr., or "Big Jake" as his friends and family call him, enters the picture. Tracing the lineage of Mauer physical dominance will bring one front and center with the patriarch of the family, Joe's grandfather. During Joe's childhood, Big Jake could be found throwing batting practice or playing a game of catch with his grandson. His fluid technique and knowing hands are relics of a once great athlete. Big Jake was a multi-sport standout at the same high school that his son and grandsons attended. At Cretin High School (later called Cretin-Derham Hall when the all-boys school Cretin merged with the all-girls school Derham), Jake Sr. was a 12-time letterman. Football was his best sport and he garnered the attention of the coaches at the University of Minnesota. Before Big Jake could begin to get his athletic career off the ground, he was drafted to serve in the Korean War. According to a Star Tribune article addressing the subject, "... and after the service his baseball career ended after just two minor league seasons when a battle with polio landed him in an iron lung. 'I lost all the weight in my legs, and I still don't walk right,' says Big Jake, 70. 'I'm just glad I'm alive. Every day I cherish it.'"

In many ways, Joe's rise to prominence is a story of family redemption. Like Ray's father in the classic, mystical baseball movie, Field of Dreams, Jake was robbed of his chance to live his dream. Fifty years later, fate had restored to his grandson in spades what was ruthlessly taken away from him. The fact that Joe would be given this opportunity while playing for his hometown team only added credence to the idea that events were being orchestrated by a divine hand: "If you build it, they will come." They must have been referring to the Quick Swing.

It was the dawn of 2001, and the Minnesota Twins were coming off a disastrous season in which they finished 69–93, dead last in their division. Nearly ten years earlier, Highland Park native Jack Morris had pitched ten innings of scoreless ball to earn the win in the seventh game of the World Series. It was their second title in four years. Attendance at the Metrodome, which once surpassed the three million threshold, now barely crossed the one million mark. The one silver lining of an awful campaign was they were rewarded with the number one pick in the amateur draft. The "twins" of the Minnesota Twins, of course, refers to the two cities of close proximity, St. Paul and Minneapolis. There, situated as one of the top prospects of the year's draft class, sat St. Paul's own Joe Mauer.

There was no way that the Twins were going to pass on the chance to take the local hero. It was exactly the kind of spark needed to reverse a recent trend of losing. There was one small catch: Mauer had to reject his scholarship offer from powerhouse Florida State and declare for the draft. The Twins nervously waited for Joe's decision. Thankfully for the Twins, Joe and his family realized the historic significance of this opportunity and permanently choose baseball over football. With the pick, Joe became one of only six Minnesota natives to have been chosen in the first round of the MLB draft. Not necessarily the hotbed for baseball recruiting (think about the weather), Joe was the first player of these six Minnesotans to go 1st overall. As if the day couldn't get any better, the Twins took Joe's older brother Jake in the 23rd round to serve as a mentor in the minors, a shrewd investment for their most coveted asset.

The drafting of Mauer signified the start of an era of consistent winning. Although Joe wouldn't reach the majors for another three years and after some of the Twins divisional championships, one can imagine the baseball gods were pleased with this turn of events. Changing the karmic influences of a sports team from negative to positive alone would have been worth the choice of Joe Mauer; just ask Cubs fans. The fact that he would become one of the elite players of his generation was simply icing on the cake.

Now that the hero storyline was established, Joe would not only have to live up to unrealistic expectations, he would have to exceed them. An 18-year-old major league prospect even of the caliber of Joe Mauer can expect to spend several years in the minors fine-tuning his abilities. This fact is more evident with catchers, Joe's natural position, as it requires a nuance and sophistication not required for most other roles on the baseball diamond. A catcher is responsible for calling a game (what type of pitch and location), managing the opponent's running game, fielding balls in his area, and calming the nerves of the pitcher. If and when Joe reached the majors, he would be asked to provide this skill set and leadership qualities to professionals who could be 15 to 20 years his senior. All this responsibility occurs before hitting a baseball, a task many experts claim is the most difficult in all of sport.

Facing this daunting proposition, how did Joe fare? After hitting .330 in the minors and showing catching instincts of a grizzled veteran, Mauer was named the starting catcher for the Minnesota Twins at the ripe age of 20. To put this in perspective, only four catchers in the history of baseball were younger when they started for their teams. On April 5, 2004, Mauer began a statistical run on the record books that continues today.

Injuries limited Joe's inaugural season, as he appeared in only 35 games. Still, his impact was widely felt in all facets of the game. He batted an impressive .308 with a .369 on base and .570 slugging percentage. The high batting average and on-base percentage would become the calling card of his career. In fact, by his third season, Joe hit a staggering .347 (while walking an additional 79 times) to lead the American League. This rate also would have placed him first in both the National and American Leagues although such an award is not recognized due to their heavily staggered schedules. The significance of the feat is considerable: in the storied history of the most immortalized of American's games, no catcher had led the American League in batting average. Only two catchers earned this title in the National League, the last doing so in 1942 when many of the elite players were serving overseas in the fight against Germany and Japan. To prove this exploit was no cosmic fluke, Joe earned another batting title two years later with a .328 average.

Mauer's career, foreshadowed by his rookie year absences, was not without major obstacles. Joe suffered a series of ailments to his knees, legs, and even had surgery for kidney blockage. Yet, the opening of the 2009 campaign offered the greatest threat to his status as one of the immortals of the game. Saddled with sacroiliac joint inflammation, a seriously painful back ailment, Joe missed the first two months of the season. Whispers of being injury prone and potentially needing a change to a position that was less physically demanding were circulating in the press and Internet blogs. Fueling this argument was the one criticism of Mauer's young career: his inability to hit for power. Since the great ones always rise to the occasion, he used these doubts to compose a season for the ages. In 138 games, Joe batted .365 with an on-base percentage of .444, answered his critics by belting 28 home runs while posting a .587 slugging percentage, and was recognized for his outstanding defense with his second straight Gold Glove. The .365 average, the highest posted by a catcher in baseball's history, garnered him his third batting title in four years and propelled him to a nearly unanimous American League Most Valuable Player Award.[14]

As for the Twins as a whole, they enjoyed one of their most exciting seasons to date. After 162 games, the Twins and Detroit Tigers were tied at the top of the American League Central standings. Per baseball rules, the two teams play one game with the winner earning the division championship and the last spot in the league playoff, while the loser goes home with its tail between its legs. Visions of repeat heartbreak danced in the minds of Twins fans everywhere as Minnesota had been faced with a similar scenario when the team lost to the Chicago White Sox in a tiebreaker game just the previous year. In front of a raucous, standing-room-only crowd, the Twins won in dramatic fashion: 6 to 5 in 12 innings. Mauer, for his efforts, reached base four times. It was the team accomplishment, however, that mattered most to Joe, not his individual game or season statistics.

During an interview with the Star Tribune, Mauer stated, "If I hit .250 and we won the World Series, I would be happier than anyone." As if Joe Mauer could possibly hit .250. This quote summarizes the additional quality that makes Mauer extraordinary. He is a family-oriented, team-first, and fan-friendly superstar. Consider an article found in a February 2010 issue of ESPN The Magazine. Ryan Hockensmith, a writer and avid baseball fan, recounts an experiment he attempted with all major sports teams in the United States. He sent a handwritten and personalized note to each team's most prominent player as well as a team's mascot and lesser known player to serve as a control. Recounting the responses he received, Hockensmith was most impressed with a postcard mailed from Joe Mauer. It reads, "Thank you for your note and kind words. I always enjoy hearing from baseball fans, and the Twins and I appreciate your support—especially in Yankees territory. I apologize for the delay in responding—with my late start to the season, I am just getting a chance to catch up on my fan mail. I hope you are having a good summer. Mine's been pretty good so far. I was voted to the All-Star Game in St. Louis. It's always an exciting 'break' from the season, and this year we got to meet the President. Now, if we can

---

14   Injuries would continue to plague Mauer in subsequent years. In 2011, he suffered through a disappointing, injury-filled campaign. He appeared in only 82 games and batted a career low .287. Combined with the fact that he just signed a new contract, fans began to become restless with his listless performance. For the first time in his career, boos could be heard throughout Target Field after he made an out. Joe experienced the Paul Bunyan syndrome in that even the mightiest of men succumb to physical limitations and growing expectations of the populace.

catch the Tigers and the White Sox for the AL Central Division title, this summer will be the best so far! Thanks again for writing, Joe."

Our family has a personal experience with the cool ease and down to earth approach Mauer has with his fan base. For you see, Darius and his wife, Jennifer, lived a Joe Mauer's throw to second base away from Joe's townhouse in St. Paul. From their window in their spare bedroom, they could often witness Joe relaxing on his elevated deck or hanging out with close friends. On one such occasion, Jennifer had a brush with greatness. It was January 24, 2010, almost at the same time that the ESPN article was published (the run date was January 28) and all of Minnesota turned their attention to the NFC Championship. The game featured the Vikings versus the New Orleans Saints. Jennifer and Darius were walking to their car, parked on the street in front of their house, to drive to a family member's house to watch the game. One aspect of Minnesota during winter time is that, with such high, accumulating snowbanks, the passenger often can't access the front door of the car from the sidewalk. Thus, Jennifer and Darius were employing their typical drill for such an occasion. Jennifer would walk up several feet to a neighbor's driveway and Darius would enter the car and make the short drive to pick her up.

Darius went to start the car and looked up to find Jennifer up the road, staring with utter awe off into the distance. Not 20 yards away was Joe Mauer, using a baseball to play an impromptu football game with a few of his buddies. Like most Minnesotans at the moment, Joe was simply killing some time before the Vikings game started. Sensing that someone was burning a hole through his chest with her eyes, Joe turned toward Jennifer and offered a wry smile and a kind wave. Still stunned and entering the car, Jennifer, a fellow Cretin-Derham alumnus in her own right, turned to her husband and said of the experience, "I can't believe Joe Mauer knows me." Darius, still new to whole concept of marriage and possibly slightly jealous, retorted, "He's Joe Mauer. If someone stares at him, he's going to wave back."

His high school friend summarized Joe's hold on the community when he was quoted by the Star Tribune as saying, "The ladies all want to be with him, and the men all want to be him." Unfortunately for all the grown men out there, you don't have the slightest chance. In fact, analyzing the résumés of the two Minnesota icons detailed in this chapter leads to an interesting question: Does your current or future offspring have a better chance becoming the next Paul Bunyan or the next Joe Mauer? If you answered the latter, you obviously would be correct. But the competition is closer than you might think. Calculating the odds of a Paul Bunyan type figure inhabiting this planet is an easy endeavor. Not even the largest person recorded in the Guinness Book of World Records, Robert Wadlow, who stood tall at 8 feet 11 inches, can even remotely challenge a man who allegedly created all the lakes in Minnesota with his footprints. The probability nudges up to the border of impossible.

But what about Joe Mauer? Are the chances of having a son that mirrors his exploits discernibly more favorable? At 18 years old, Joe stood at 6 feet 4 inches and held a national record for most consecutive games with at least one home run. Yet, according to his high school coach, Jim O'Neal, he could rarely be found in the weight room. Think of the list of "firsts" described above that were accomplished by Mauer, including the first high school athlete to be named USA Today player of the year in both football and baseball, the first Minnesotan drafted first overall in the MLB draft, the first catcher in 104 years to win an American League batting title, the first to do it twice, and the first to do it three times. Throw in the fact that he is playing in the same city he grew up in, that he is also a league MVP, by all accounts is a nice guy in an era of prima donna athletes, and I say you are just as likely to need a wagon for a cradle as you are achieving these same results.

The obvious difference between Joe Mauer and Paul Bunyan is that we believe deep in our hearts we could be like Joe. After all, he grew up in a middle class, heart of America town; he liked to play ball in his backyard; he doesn't want to pay more than $17 for a haircut; he can be a regular homebody; and he can even get shy around pretty girls. How is that different from half the male population in the United States?

The fact of the matter is, as similar as we might be to Mr. Mauer, we couldn't be more different. Joe Mauer is an extreme statistical anomaly, a Haley's Comet of the sporting world. He is the product of superior genetics, an unparalleled commitment and work ethic, and the perfect environmental factors that fostered his development. If Joe Mauer wasn't such a rare gem, why then would a billionaire not prone to throwing away his vast fortune away commit $184 million of his own money by signing Joe to an eight-year contract unprecedented in franchise history? Because the family of former Minnesota Twins owner Carl Pohlad (he died in 2009) realized that they will never encounter in their lifetime a more perfect representative for the health and wellbeing of their ball club.

Being Joe Mauer is an unattainable goal for the 99% ... and that is what makes him so special. This idea may not seem so groundbreaking, and yet it doesn't stop parents in youth leagues from yelling at the coaches when their son and, increasingly, their daughter doesn't receive enough playing time. It is the parents' strong belief, one that they are willing to fight for, that external factors like the coach's preference for another player and not their offspring's natural ability are holding them back from greatness. This concept is known as the fundamental attribution error or correspondence error. Psychologist Lee Ross[15] first used the term to describe a phenomenon he had witnessed in his research. When evaluating other people, humans are more likely to attribute another's actions and behaviors to internal qualities within the person. When evaluating oneself, context and situational factors are more heavily considered.

Expounding upon the example from above, let's say there are two youth baseball players who spend most of the game on the bench. The parent of one of the children may likely have two completely different sets of reasoning for this occurrence. In evaluating the player who isn't his child, the father may focus on the youth's poor hitting, weak arm, and lack of in-game knowledge. In examining his son, he may focus on the fact that his kid is from a different neighborhood than many of the players the coaches tend to play more regularly.

Fundamental attribution error provides substantial ego protection and allows an individual to ignore information that may be too difficult to accept. This self-interest is humans' driving force, according to American sociologist Gerhard Lenski, who claims, "When men are confronted with important decisions where they are obliged to choose between their own, or their group's, interest and the interests of others, they nearly always choose the former—although often seeking to hide this fact from themselves and others."[16] One person's livelihood and wellbeing is all too often dependent on someone else's marginalization and oppression, and we obscure our fellow man's humanity with our protective, self-exalting views of ourselves.

For instance, many ambitious parents are unwilling to accept the astronomical odds of achieving lasting success and the financial rewards that come with an athletic career. Recent studies conclude that over 41 million youth play in at least one organized sport. According to the Little League Baseball Organization, 2.2 million of those youth play baseball every year. Major League Baseball has 750 players on their current roster. Of these

15   Ross L. The intuitive psychologist and his shortcomings. In L. Berkowitz (ed.), *Advances in Experimental Social Psychology* (Vol. 10, pp. 173–220). New York: Academic, 1977.

16   Lenski GE. *Power and Privilege: A Theory of Social Stratification.* Chapel Hill: The University of North Carolina Press, 1984.

750 players on the opening day of the 2010 season, 231 were foreign born. In essence, 2.2 million children and adolescents are competing for 529 seats at the table. Unless their child is more skilled than the equivalent of their nearest 40,000 peers, it might be time for parents to start emphasizing the importance of their child's reading and math skills. Despite this overwhelming evidence to the contrary, Mark Hyman points out in his book dedicated to the topic that 40 percent of parents believe their son or daughter will play a sport in college.[17] Six percent of parents claim their child is destined for the professional level, or 2,400 times more likely than the actual occurrence.

Not surprisingly, the effects of fundamental attribution error are stronger and more prevalently found in societies that promote individualism. Individualism is a concept worn like a badge of honor in the United States. This idea brings us full circle to the quote found at the beginning of this chapter and the question of the founding fathers' intentions alluded to earlier. The most celebrated line in the Declaration of Independence, "We hold these truths to be self-evident, that all men are created equal," is the foundation of our American identity. The notion of a fundamental equality has unified people under a common deity, rallied people for political change, and convinced people to help one another in times of crisis.

Does, however, the notion of "all men are created equal" actually have any scientific or practical merit? Brushing aside the reality that women and people of color were excluded from that statement and updating it to a more modern context, are we really all that equal? From the moment we are born, our physical attributes are charted and then compared to the height and weight of "average" infants. The national physical fitness test administered at most elementary schools examines a youth's speed, agility, and flexibility and rewards those with superior qualities. Every high school and college class has a valedictorian, and each graduate can be rank ordered in terms of academic performance. Top-rated reality programming thrives on creating scenarios to test the attributes of selected contestants, with only the "best" surviving.

The irony is that a society founded on the idea that everyone is equal is constantly creating new and improved means to demonstrate we are wholly unequal. We should all be thankful for the resulting difference. Nature, in its infinite wisdom, has given the human species the genetic capacity for significant diversity. Some are more gifted at artistic expression, others at cooking, while a few can use geometric principles to construct a skyscrap-

17   Hyman M. *Until It Hurts: America's Obsession with Youth Sports and How It Harms Our Kids.* Boston: Beacon Press, 2010.

er. Some will be able to dunk a basketball on a regulation rim, while others will be able to dissect James Joyce's Ulysses. The more heterogeneous a species, that is, the more diversity, the more likely said species will thrive. Homogeneity, in contrast, is a recipe for early extinction.

Even the man credited with writing the words "all men are created equal" hardly has any peers. Jefferson was a lawyer, philosopher, statesman, and inventor. He acquired a basic understanding of French, Latin, and Greek. His devotion to lifelong learning led to the founding of the University of Virginia and his political acumen paved the way for the purchase of the Louisiana Territory that more than doubled the land area of the United States. He lived in a mansion on an awe inspiring estate and he owned several slaves. He was both ally and rival to Alexander Hamilton and George Washington. In his lifetime, he held the position of Minister to France, Governor of Virginia, the first Secretary of State, Vice President, and President of the United States. Not quite the same curriculum vitae most of us are able to submit when applying for a job opening.

Such examples demonstrate the absurdity of holding on to the belief that we are all the same. Don't blame Jefferson, however, for misleading you into a false sense of superiority. Nor should you assume that the claims in the Declaration of Independence are flawed. We stop at "all men were created equal" and proceed accordingly. The full line reads, "We hold these truths to be self-evident, that all men are created equal, that they are endowed by their Creator with certain unalienable Rights, that among these are Life, Liberty and the pursuit of Happiness." As with many themes, ideas, and sayings, we have taken this passage out of context. We are not equal because we have the same makeup, abilities, talents, and fortitude. We are all equal because our birth gives us each the God-given right to life, liberty, and the pursuit of happiness. We are equal in that each of us has universal needs and hopes—such as access to clean drinking water, freedom from oppression, the safety of our children, and the preservation of our human dignity, no matter our status or circumstance. A no less revolutionary proclamation, though still misinterpreted. And a no less difficult standard for a society to attempt, and oftentimes fail, to maintain.

Joe Mauer is everyone's equal not because he has the same biological attributes as you and I. He is the same because, as a member of American society, no one can obstruct his right to life, the liberties afforded to him by the U.S. Constitution and the laws of the land, or his pursuit of happiness however he may define this concept. He will not be restricted from showcasing his baseball abilities due to the fact that he was born into the middle class and is not of noble blood. He will not be forced to quit if he designates himself a Christian, Muslim, or Jew. If one party rules the government, he won't be relegated to the bench because of any political affiliation. He will simply be judged on his merits and contributions to his designated profession. Tomorrow, he could decide to hang up his cleats for good and pursue a different path toward happiness. No one can stop him; just as no one should be able to stop us from attempting this same journey. It just so happens that his pursuit of happiness nets him $23 million a year, unlimited access to the most coveted of resources, and the admiration of millions of people around the world. It is pivotal to remember, however, that the rest of us are unlikely to be so fortunate.

Power Points

- The prominent inclusion of Paul Bunyan in American *folklore* indicates a society that values hard work, perseverance, and mastery over their environment.

- While Paul Bunyan is a man of *legend* and Joe Mauer is a man in St. Paul, the likelihood of raising a son to be like either one of them is about the same.

- The *fundamental attribution error* allows an individual to blame erroneous environmental factors for his or her performance letdowns while ignoring the limitations of his or her biological endowment.

- People in societies that promote *individualism* are more susceptible to the *fundamental attribution error* and are more likely to have inflated expectations for success.

- The Declaration of Independence champions *equality* through *life, liberty*, and the *pursuit of happiness* and should not be misconstrued as the belief that our founding fathers believed everyone was created equal.

Next Destination

The quest for a just and equitable society is paramount for leveling the playing field of opportunity, but no rule of law can close the biological endowment gap.

4

Engineering the Great Society

Rule of the Road: Governments cannot legislate genetics.

Mile Markers: Citizenship, Voting Rights, Slavery, Constitution, 3/5^ths Compromise, United Nations, Civil Rights Act, Title IX, Women in Education, Milton Friedman, Olympics, Rafer Johnson, NFL Draft, Self-Schema, Expectations, Disillusionment, Biological Ceilings

Jefferson City, only 30 minutes from my adopted home of Columbia, was no stranger to me. Many times, I had made the climb up the state capitol building's white steps to gaze upon the murals lining the rotunda depicting important moments in Missouri history. With my wife and three-year-old child accompanying me, however, this visit was different. This day was personal. Standing in front of a black-robed judge in this house of democracy, I took the oath to become a United States citizen. What my spouse and son had gained as a birthright, I had achieved through an elaborate process set forth by the U.S. State Department. The rules of the day required a wait of five years after receiving my green card to apply for full citizenship. Since my card arrived in 1971, it set me up for an historical happenstance: I would become eligible for this honor in 1976. The significance was not lost on me or the nearly 100 people who joined me in taking this oath. As we congratulated one another, complete strangers embarking upon the American dream, we reflected on our good fortune to complete this journey in the year the United States was celebrating its bicentennial.

Later that fall, I exercised one of my newly established rights. Standing in line at Fairview Elementary School, I cast my vote in the election pitting Jimmy Carter against Gerald Ford. I remember paying extra attention to the diversity of people engaging in this act. If you don't vote by mail, the next time you queue up waiting to fill out your ballot, I encourage you to also take a look at the composition of your fellow voters. I can safely assume that it will be made up of men and women of a variety of races, some born in the United States, others from countries around the world. Some will be well-to-do and own their homes; others will live on someone else's land and have little prospect for work or savings. We can also assume that a large portion of the population will be absent from this line because they choose not to participate. In national elections during a presidential year, voter turnout will barely exceed 50%, whereas in years where the next commander-in-chief is not on the ballot, turnout is almost always less than 40%.

Maybe if we all had a better understanding of the evolution of suffrage and the efforts to allow such a broad swath of Americans the opportunity to engage in this civil process, the right to vote would not be taken so much for granted. During the time of the inking of the Declaration of Independence in 1776 and later, the ratification of the Constitution in 1787, women and people of color were not allowed to vote (although in four states, freed slaves were allowed). White men who did not own property were also excluded. In some states, there were religious tests not only for the privilege to vote but also to hold political office.

From a contemporary perspective, these restrictions certainly pour cold water on the principles of equality and the right to pursue liberty advocated in the Declaration of Independence. However, no issue served more to undermine the radical and revolutionary principles of our most cherished and historic documents than the treatment of the African slave. That is not to say there didn't exist loud voices decrying this horrific practice. In fact, an early draft of the Declaration of Independence listed this grievance:

"He [King George III] has waged cruel war against human nature itself, violating its most sacred rights of life and liberty in the persons of a distant people who never offended him, captivating and carrying them into slavery in another hemisphere, or to incur miserable death in their transportation hither. This piratical warfare, the opprobrium of infidel powers, is the warfare of the Christian king of Great Britain.... [determined to keep open a market where MEN should be bought and sold,] he has prostituted his negative for suppressing every legislative attempt to prohibit or to restrain this execrable commerce."[18]

Jefferson doesn't mince words regarding the abhorrence of slavery; it represents a high profile example of how many of the founding fathers recognized the hypocrisy of a burgeoning government promoting equality while accepting the enslavement of a people. Unfortunately, many of the framers of the document had a vested interest in slavery and viewed this statement as an accusation not only against the king but also against themselves. How could they criticize the king for this action when they condoned the system? Faced with losing a large contingent of supporters, this grievance was left out of the final draft. One can only imagine how the alternative choice of including this objection in the Declaration of Independence may have shaped history differently.

Instead, the issue of slavery housed within a democracy continued to plague the framers of the Constitution when facing the issue of taxation and representation. Southern states wanted slaves to be counted in their census and thus increase the proportion of seats in the House of Representatives. Thus, they unabashedly supported the idea of blacks being included in their numbers for proposals to widen their influence while working to ensure these same people would be barred from the opportunity to send their representatives to Congress. Naturally, not everyone was on board with the proposal and a compromise was approved: Slaves would count as "3/5 of all other persons." If being forbidden the right to vote wasn't defaming enough, now black slaves in this country were considered less than a whole person.

In retrospect, many of today's teachers and historians have attempted to debunk the egalitarian and infallible mythos of our early leaders. With the record described above, and even without touching on the plight of Native Americans, immigrant populations, and women of all races, they certainly have a valid argument. It is just as important, however, to understand the cultural and political context in which they were operating. Here were 13 loosely affiliated states with competing motivations and agendas attempting to create a fledging nation. Distrustful of powerful, central governments, coming up with agreed upon rules and regulations was an uphill battle. Many of the big-picture questions that would threaten to break

---

18   America's Principles in Public Policy. Retrieved November 14, 2014 from http://
      www.americasprinciples.com/home/thomas-jefferson-he-has-waged-cruel-war-
      against-human-nature-itself-violating-its-most-sacred-rights-of-life-and-liberty

up this alliance, such as slavery, were put on the back burner. While our founding fathers' record on human rights was certainly mixed, their genius came in the form of a legal document that could be changed and address the contentious issues as circumstances and viewpoints evolved. In fact, of the 17 Constitutional Amendments enacted in the more than 200 years since the Bill of Rights was ratified, nine either directly increased the number of people allowed to vote, eliminated slavery and similar practices, or widened the scope of who was protected by the laws of the land.

This commitment to inclusion remains the legacy of the American experiment: A government's primary purpose is to protect the rights of its citizens and promote their opportunities for success.

This concept has had immense influence on the countries of the world and how their citizens choose to be governed. Laws that mandate equal opportunity find a framework in Article 25 of the Universal Human Rights Declaration, adopted by the United Nations in 1948, which states, "Everyone has a right to a standard of living adequate for the health and well-being of himself and his family, including food, clothing, housing and medical care and necessary social services, and the right to security in the event of unemployment, sickness, disability, widowhood, old age or other lack of livelihood." [19]

To that end, modern societies have policies in place that address the treatment of their most vulnerable and maligned inhabitants. United States hospitals must provide all necessary stabilizing treatment for a person in need of emergency medical treatment or who is in labor, regardless of citizenship status or ability to pay. Australia and Canada prohibit workplace discrimination based on a person's sexual orientation, among other categories. Japan's 1992 Child Care Leave Law allows male or female full-time regular employees to take a leave of absence until their child reaches one year of age. In nations with such laws, excluding a person from these benefits can result in public outcry, litigation, government penalties, and political shame.

Sweeping reforms such as the Civil Rights Act of 1964, prohibiting discrimination in the American workplace based on race, color, religion, gender, or national origin, have had an immense effect in expanding the boundaries of equality that even the framers of the Constitution could not have conceived. Consider its impact on women attending an institution of higher learning. Before the 1960s, few women believed college attendance was a possibility. For those who made this choice, their options were often

19   United Nations. The Universal Declaration of Human Rights. Retrieved November 14, 2014 from http://www.un.org/en/documents/udhr/

limited to the strictly women's colleges scattered across the country. While the Civil Rights Act of 1964 began to pave the road for more women to have access to higher education, the Title IX law served as a superhighway for this endeavor. Title IX states, "No person in the United States shall, on the basis of sex, be excluded from participation in, be denied benefits of, or be subjected to discrimination under any education program or activity receiving Federal financial assistance."[20]

At the advent of Title IX, some colleges and universities had already adapted their policies and approaches to cater to an influx of young women seeking further education. For those who were slower to change with the times, the potential of being denied federal funding cajoled them into making the necessary transformation. Once these gates were open, women have never looked back. According to statistics kept by the U.S. Department of Labor, by 1980 more women began enrolling in college than men. Since 1984, more women have attended universities seeking a graduate degree than men. Today, 57% of college graduates are women. The number of minorities attending college has followed a similar (if not quite as drastic) increase. As a result, women, minorities, and openly gay individuals now occupy the highest positions in Fortune 500 companies, the most prestigious educational institutions, and all facets of government. The most salient example of this revolutionary trend was the 2008 election of an African American President of the United States, an inconceivable notion in the 1950s and '60s.

With governments addressing preexisting limits to equality and actively attempting to level the playing field, why do we still find such varying incomes, status, and possessions among people as described in Chapter 1? Nobel prize-winning economist Milton Friedman says it's because legislation targets the wrong obstacle to a fair chance at societal success. According to him, laws afford "equality of opportunity in the sense that no one should be prevented by arbitrary obstacles from using his capacities to pursue his own objectives." However, the elimination of arbitrary obstacles does nothing to remove biological ones. According to Paul Kalra, author of The American Class System: Divide and Rule[21], Friedman's voluminous works declare that "equality of outcomes is an impossible dream because abilities are not equally distributed."

---

20   U.S. Department of Education. Title IX and Sex Discrimination. Retrieved November 14, 2014 from http://www2.ed.gov/about/offices/list/ocr/docs/tix_dis.html

21   Kalra P. *The American Class System: Divide and Rule*. Brooklyn: Antenna Books, 1996.

While Friedman may be accused of failing to appreciate the extreme complexities of equality and injustice, rooted in his argument is an important point. Despite the existence of equal opportunity laws and practices, many people are still denied equal opportunity every day. Not by a realtor, job interviewer, or college admissions officer acting on racist, sexist, classist, or other prejudicial impulses—as we have great historical reason to suspect—but by our very own natural biodiversity. It turns out that neatly defined equal opportunity legislation is not sufficient to address the fact that each person is born equipped with an entirely unique—and inherently unequal—set of biological endowments. These physical, mental, and emotional traits can pose advantages or disadvantages, rendering us skillful or inept at certain tasks and prone to others' praise or disdain. They include things from hair color and height to charisma and intellect. Duke University philosophy professor Alex Rose calls these traits "immutable and inevitable," emphasizing the finality of their presence in our genetic makeup. Since we cannot change or refuse these traits, we're faced with a wondrous benefit or a perpetual handicap—both beyond our control.

Although the consequences of our biological endowments are unique for each person, perhaps the one universal effect they have is to nullify equal opportunity, a claim Friedman has made for much of the latter half of the 20th century. Simply put, people approach any given prospect with a spectrum of dissimilarities that affect how well they will capitalize on an opportunity. While equal opportunity legislation effectively opens many doors, there is still the matter of getting to and through those doors. To reach an open door to success, some have to travel a long distance, while others barely walk a mile. Some must battle through wind and rain, while yet others are conveyed to the door by a sheltered, moving sidewalk. Some are too large to fit through the width of the frame, no matter how they squeeze and bend, while others are too short to reach the knob.

This fact does not diminish the idea that the door simply being open serves as a great benefit. For many people prior to the advent of equal opportunity, that same door was closed, locked, and potentially electrified. The problem remains that though biological endowments cannot be legally used as reason to shut the door, they have everything to do with our reaching the door and passing through it. As shown by the metaphorical factors above, an unusable and unreachable door can be as useless as a closed or locked one. Yet many a person has had this same disappointing experience with the premise of equal opportunity because of the limitations caused by their biological endowments.

Let me make something abundantly clear, however: There is nothing wrong with holding on to a dream even if it is a long shot based on your genetics. In fact, when I was eight, I dared to dream big as well.

I grew up in India during a time of great change and social upheaval. During my first ten years of life, World War II began and concluded, Mahatma Gandhi reached his apex (leading to his eventual death), the British abandoned rule of the country, and Pakistan became an independent nation. It also was an era of intense violence in the region sparked by numerous communal riots. Gunfire, explosions, and the cries of those who lost loved ones were the constant background noise surrounding my family home. My parents, older brother, and sisters were remarkable in their ability to insulate me from the troubles that brewed all around us. I also developed my own strategies to shield myself mentally and emotionally from any dangers that might have been lurking. In impromptu races with my friends, I had established myself as the fastest eight-year-old in the neighborhood. This fact fueled my greatest defense, a fantasy in which I firmly believed in my capacity to outrun any terrorist, gunman, or any other identifiable bad guy.

As the hostilities progressed, makeshift markets began to spring up, selling whatever food merchants could come by. This included leftover army rations from World War II. With my father occupied with the task of securing an exit plan for the family, a volunteer was needed to retrieve sustenance for the household. I viewed myself as the perfect candidate and such a task had the added benefit of showcasing my quickness. With very few options, my mother reluctantly agreed. I turned my weekly runs to the marketplace into a game, dodging in and out of alleyways and timing myself in hopes of setting a new personal record. In setting these records, I imagined that I was the great Jessie Owens. Even though Owens was an American, he was a hero to many people across the world. His exploits were transcendent: a man who stood up to the Nazi machine and shattered the ideology of Aryan supremacy. His exploits helped cultivate a lifelong fascination with the Olympic Games. When I ran in and out of the marketplace, I pictured myself in the starting blocks during an Olympic race and beating everyone to the finish line.

Eventually, my family was able to join my grandmother who had migrated to the newly formed Pakistan. While it was difficult to leave our home and the friends that we had established in India, life settled down for all members of the family, and we enjoyed relative peace. In our haste to reach safety, we were forced to leave behind most of our furniture, clothes, and other possessions. One item I was able to carry with me from India was my gift of speed. I would spend a great deal of my adolescent life finding new and increasingly elaborate venues to test this talent.

Any burgeoning Pakistani athlete begins by playing the country's two national sports, field hockey and cricket. In cricket, I used to be an opening batsman. This requires good eye-hand coordination to hit the fast ball. In hockey, I played the right wing position that requires quickness and ability to carry a hard ball with a stick curved at the bottom as one weaves through defenders. I was a member of the community team, Ghazvani Club, and commitment to this sport meant practices every night, with games played all day Sunday.

As college approached, the competition was stiffer in cricket and hockey and required me to devote more time honing my craft. Pakistan was and continues to be a world powerhouse in these sports. Like many high stakes, high reward affairs in fledgling Pakistan, politics and nepotism dominated all proceedings of these teams. For these reasons, I decided to cut out the middleman. Besides, why complicate matters with bats, balls, and sticks when the act of running was my true passion? I turned my attention to track and field with a focus on the sprinting events.

The added benefit of choosing track and field was that it is mainly an individual endeavor. Since I was also pursuing my medical degree, I needed an athletic activity that allowed for a flexible schedule, one not dependent on the availabilities of other people. I remember this time as some of the most challenging and exhilarating days of my life. A typical day consisted of attending classes from 8 a.m. to 3 p.m. I would come home and take a power nap for usually 30 to 60 minutes and go to the stadium to do my training for a couple of hours. A few of my colleagues would join in, and soon a tight-knit group of four was formed: Talib, Ghanchi, Jaleel, and I. After training and cleaning ourselves up, we would walk downtown and sit in a cafe for tea and patties, another remnant of British rule. By 8 p.m., I would return home for a modest, economical, and easy-to-cook dinner. From 10 p.m. to 3 a.m., we would get together again for group study of medicine. Bedtime would be around 3:30 a.m., and the morning would arrive quickly and abruptly at 7:30 a.m. when I would begin the routine once again.

This devotion led to immediate success. There were several levels of competition that I was preparing for all year. The most coveted and prestigious was the annual sports event of Dow Medical College that attracted numerous participants in the area. The event lasted for three days, and students competed in all the standard track and field events. My standards were the 100-, 200-, and 400-meter races; the long jump; the hop, step, and jump (better known today as triple jump); and the anchor of the 4 x 100 relay. Every year, I won each of these events, often breaking records of my own creation. A champion was declared, based on the highest number of events won by an individual. I won this championship for the five consecutive years I was in medical school. As a result, I was awarded the college color in track and field every year of my stay in the medical college.

My local exploits created opportunities to compete at the national level in the form of the annual intercollegiate track and field meet. This competition was organized by the University of Karachi, and I faced higher quality athletes from various other colleges under the Karachi University system. At this level, I needed to narrow my focus to the 100 meters, 200 meters, and long jump. The results were the same: victory in every event. As a winner of this intercollegiate competition, I was selected to represent Karachi University in the annual interuniversity sports. These are equivalent to NCAA sports in the United States. Wearing the banner of Karachi University, I would often compete with the very best in the nation (a country drawing from nearly 60 million people) in the 100 meters, 200 meters, and 4 x 100 relay. As a result, I was invited to train with the Pakistani national team. It was then, kneeling side by side with the world's greatest sprinters, I started to believe that the Olympic dream I imagined as an eight-year-old in a New Delhi marketplace could become a reality.

At this level of competition, I would be required to invest all my time and energy in this pursuit. It also would require me to temporarily abandon my studies of medicine. The payoff would be a chance to qualify for the 1960 Olympics held in Rome. As I pondered this decision, one that would dictate the immediate course of my life and possibly shift it in an ultimate direction, a visitor arrived at our training complex. His name was Rafer Johnson, an American decathlete who had won the silver medal in the 1952 Olympics. He came to Pakistan as part of a student ambassador program. The moment Rafer walked into the room, the part of my brain that formed the concept of an Olympic athlete became permanently rewired. While gracious and humble by nature, he stood at an imposing 6'3" and weighed 230 pounds. Contrast that with my 5'7", 150 pound frame, and you can imagine my disillusionment. I felt like a Lilliputian who had met Gulliver for the first time.

Rafer was instrumental in updating our training methods, most notably introducing us to the importance of weight training. Most important, his presence served as a catalyst for a choice I have never regretted. It takes a man like Rafer Johnson to win an Olympic gold medal: While his towering athleticism was best suited for track and field, he was a starter on Coach John Wooden's 1959–60 UCLA basketball team and was even drafted by the NFL despite the fact he didn't play college football. For proof of his superior genetic background, one would have to look no further than his brother, who had a Hall of Fame career in the NFL, or his daughter, a 2000 Olympic competitor in beach volleyball. Two years after he came to Pakistan, Rafer would beat out training partner and good friend C. Y. Yang for the gold medal in the decathlon at the Rome Olympics.

The moment Rafer entered my life, I knew my Olympic dream had ended. My sprinting career came to a self-imposed, abrupt end. From that point forward, my personal path was clearly charted. I would become Syed Arshad Husain, M.D. Soon, even the remnants of this athletic venture began to fade from view. The numerous trophies, medals, and ribbons I had garnered throughout the years had been appropriated by my younger siblings. They would hold local competitions among their friends in the neighborhood and crown the winners with my hard earned awards.

I certainly wasn't the first local star athlete who fell victim to his or her biological limitations. A few years ago, I had the chance to watch this obsession with genetic endowments play out before my eyes. Chase Daniel, a former star quarterback of my hometown Missouri Tigers, stands a relatively short 6 feet in a sport with a soft spot for tall quarterbacks. Thus, he was bypassed in the NFL draft, despite holding 34 MU football records; throwing for 12,515 yards; completing 101 touchdowns to only 41 interceptions, with a 68% completion rate; and having a superior quarterback rating of 148.95. In fact, a 2008 ESPN Magazine article entitled, "Only the Name is the Same," predicted the struggles Daniel would have convincing NFL scouts and GMs that his flashy statistics could translate to the pro game. The article's author, Seth Wickersham, went as far as contrasting the relatively squat Daniel with his statuesque teammate Chase Patton to illustrate his point. Wickersham claimed that at 6'4", Patton stood a better chance than Daniel at getting drafted, despite not having "started a game since high school and in his four years at Mizzou [having] completed [only] 16 of 26 passes with one interception."

A year after the story was published, Wickersham was proven to be partially correct. As stated earlier, Mr. Daniel went undrafted and currently sees limited game action with the Kansas City Chiefs. Mr. Patton, on the other hand, never was able to broker his physical superiority into an

NFL contract, demonstrating, like equities traded on the New York Stock Exchange, the up-and-down volatility of professional sports.

With the journey to stardom fraught with so many pitfalls, obstacles, and variables like height outside the control of the individual, how are parents supposed to respond when their child exhibits a natural talent or develops an interest in a specific area such as art, sports, music, or academics? Should they extinguish their fascination with science because they are unlikely to become Albert Einstein, Marie Curie, or Stephen Hawking? Should they discourage their love of music because the Justin Timberlakes and Alicia Keys of the world are as rare as the Yangtze River dolphin[22]? The simple answer is to encourage and help cultivate this gift with all available resources. Having a dream or even the shedding of blood, sweat, and tears to realize that dream is not the problem. It is the unrealistic expectations and initial definition of success that is the root of dissatisfaction.

The psychological concept of self-schema helps shed light on these issues. Self-schemas are the thoughts, beliefs, and ideas that we form about ourselves. A person who is able to paint a picture that other people view as being desirable may adopt the self-schema of "artist." This personal label could also dictate a range of behaviors. For instance, people with the self-schema of "artist" might invest in studio space to practice their craft. One's self-schema plays an important role in the formation of expectations and the subsequent emotions one experiences when faced with feedback. Let's say two people paint an identical landscape with every brush stroke and every detail also being identical. Both are hung on the walls of separate galleries. Let's also pretend that as people walk by these paintings, they give equally harsh reviews. The only difference is that one of the painters holds the self-schema of artist while the other sees herself as a hobbyist painter. Guess which one is more likely to shrug off the criticism and which one might need a full box of Girl Scout cookies and a bottle of wine to begin to ease the pain?

When dealing with strong self-schemas about ourselves, we often imagine the best case scenario without considering the most likely outcomes. In turn, we mistakenly set such a high standard for achieving success that failure is all but a given. An individual who deems himself an

---

22 Considered an omen of fortune and good luck among fisherman of the region, the Yangtze River dolphins once numbered in the thousands as early as the 1950s. Since then, the population has seen a rapid decline. In 2007, a scientist led an extensive six week search to determine their current numbers. Their best efforts failed to uncover a single specimen, leading to speculation that the Yangtze River dolphin may be extinct.

artist may only reach a state of satisfaction if his work is received well by critics, hangs in a prestigious museum, or is purchased for a reasonable sum of money. Yet, if we remember the bell curve, these outcomes fall into the far right tail and represent a very small probability of occurring. More likely, an artist will paint a picture, and her friends and family will sincerely tell her how great it is and that she possesses a unique talent.

A perfect example of a parent setting a reasonable expectation and re-defining success occurred just recently when I was visiting a friend. After a nice dinner, my friend asked her seven-year-old daughter to sing us a song she recently learned. The young girl took a little bit of encouragement to overcome her shyness, but from the first note, I could tell she had a lovely voice. Once she concluded, I stood up and applauded her performance. I said, "You really sounded great, you should sing in your school choir."

Obviously satisfied with my response, she shouted in a high pitch characteristic of seven-year-old girls, "I want to be sooo famous. I want to be famous sooooo bad, I can hardly stand it."

Without missing a beat, her mother stepped in and said, "Honey, if you continue to practice, your singing will bring joy to people around you, including yourself." She went on to say, "I don't think if I could wave a magic wand that I would want to make you famous." Then she turned to me and finished with, "Nor would I necessarily wish that on anyone I loved."

With these words, my friend addressed three important themes with her daughter in regard to her singing ability. First, she defined the reasonable measure of success for her daughter as bringing "joy to the people around her, including yourself." Second, by equating the achievement of fame with magic, she highlighted how this expectation was rooted in fantasy. Third, in the unlikely event her daughter did become famous, this outcome didn't forecast a happy or fulfilling life. Without continuous reinforcement of these themes, my friend's daughter could experience disillusionment if she developed the self-schema of "singer" and failed to be considered famous.

This same type of disillusionment could have easily overtaken me the day Rafer Johnson was introduced to my life. In reality, however, it became one of the best things to happen to me. It allowed me to move away from the self-schema of "athlete" and firmly focus on another of my fully formed schemas of "academic." It propelled me to seek out the best possible medical education, a journey that led to exciting adventures in London, Montreal, and New York City. However, it did take a long time for my acquaintances to stop referring to me as "Arshad the athlete" and change to "Arshad the professor." Before long, I greatly preferred the latter.

With this additional schema as a fundamental part of my identity, I was able to quickly wipe away any bitterness and view my athletic career with a great deal of fondness and satisfaction. After all, being a recognized athlete allowed me to move around and become comfortable with a diverse group of individuals from all spheres of life. My early success in sprinting helped me form positive self-esteem as a young man. Sports and belonging to a team of peers with common goals offered me lessons in self-discipline, respect for playing by the rules, loyalty, camaraderie, and the ability to accept adversity and defeat with dignity. No doubt regular exercise and good nourishment also provide a foundation for a good health. Every one of these skills I have called upon in becoming a medical director and in the formation of my nonprofit organization.

Most important, I had a really good time running track. Any time that eight-year-old boy reminds me of the dream I once possessed, I have satiated my athletic desire by attending the Olympics in Montreal, Los Angeles, Barcelona, and Atlanta and watching the truly great performers display their gifts. By sharing my trophies and awards with my younger siblings, they, too, could engage in healthy fantasies of Olympic glory.

I owe my mother and father a measure of thanks for insisting that I develop multiple facets to my sense of self. While they were supportive of athletics, they made sure these pursuits did not interfere with education or my responsibility to be a good citizen in my community. Similarly, my wife and I attempted to raise our sons with multiple self-schemas. Even though my youngest son identified strongly with the sport of soccer and competed year-round for most of his childhood, his self-schemas of "academic," "singer," "helper," and "writer" proved vital during his transition from high school. Recruited to play soccer by a few small colleges, a back injury forced him to sit out training camp his freshman year. Once he was fully healed, he decided soccer was no longer a priority and he has never looked back. Conversely, if I had overemphasized the schema of "athlete" in an ill-fated attempt to restore my lost glory, imagine the discontent my son would experience with the conclusion of his sports career.

In essence, the adoption of multiple schemas serves as a means of hedging your bets, like buying gold in times of high inflation. As a coping skill to our ever-changing surroundings, multiple schemas allow for a variety of pursuits once the limit of a biological talent is discovered or exploited. Chase Patton employed that strategy during his college years at the University of Missouri. Thankfully, he didn't count on the prognostications of sports writers who trumpeted his NFL prospects and took full advantage of his free education. When his number went uncalled during draft day, his dedication to his studies allowed him to become a dentist without skipping a beat. Even the great Rafer Johnson benefited from maintaining multiple schemas. Athletes' means of livelihood comes to an end well before the halfway point of their lives. Drawing from the lessons taught to him by his family and undoubtedly his basketball coach, John Wooden, Rafer dedicated himself to becoming a well-rounded individual. Once his decathlon days were over, he was able to have a successful career as a film actor, a member of the Peace Corps, a political campaign volunteer, a sportscaster, and an avid supporter of the Special Olympics.

In the end, all humans hit a ceiling when it comes to biological endowments. The bodies or minds of the great ones will eventually betray them, and a younger, fresher, and more inspired person will take their place. Despite myriad strategies a society employs to maintain an aura of "equal opportunity," this beloved concept will never be a guarantee in part because biological endowments cannot be regulated or legislated. While a just society hopes to provide equal opportunity for its citizens in order to benefit from what is equally available, a person must possess the biological endowments that lead them to enshrinement among the 1%.

As a free people, we must continue to press our elected leaders to tackle environmental dissimilarities and circumstantial discriminations that decrease the probability individuals will reach their potential. I am pleased, however, that governments are unable to address inequality at the DNA level. The "greats" should be allowed to flourish and be admired. Their exploits should fill the dreams and imaginations of the next generation. At the same time, the 99% cannot afford to turn a blind eye to the role of biological endowments in determining elite success. We also must not be discouraged because our strengths don't mirror what is popular or generously rewarded. It does no good for parents, teachers, and mass media to encourage people to aspire only to goals a few genetically predestined people will reach. All individuals must be guided to discover and develop their own unique traits. Only when we place ridiculous expectations on ourselves, jamming our square-peg endowments into the round-hole occupations that indulge our unrealistic self-schemas, do we become burdened by our lack of success.

In the upcoming chapters, we will examine sources of this discontent and why many people waste time, money, and effort in pursuit of dreams that aren't really theirs in the first place, believing wholeheartedly in a string of falsehoods—the promise of fortune and happiness—that discount the power of their predetermined genetics. In this world of variable chances, the truly level playing field belongs to those who are capitalizing on their unique biological endowments. Nonetheless, they, too, discover that the door to those opportunities few of us will ever encounter is slowly closing.

Power Points

- Spirited by a *Constitution* fashioned to adapt to changes in societal norms and public opinion, race, gender, sexual orientation, and socioeconomic status are no longer absolute deterrents for individuals to reach the upper echelons of their desired professions.

- Despite significant advancements spurred by such legislation as *the Civil Rights Act* and *Title IX* to limit discrimination, laws are not designed to balance nor are they capable of balancing the inequality associated with differences in biological endowment.

- *Self-schemas* are a series of terms, characteristics, and labels with which an individual strongly identifies and which helps form a major component of identity.

- Developing multiple *self-schemas* allows individuals to adjust to life circumstances and increases the likelihood of enduring the inevitable collision into one's *biological ceiling*.

- Opportunities afforded by a just and equitable society are still best exploited by those with superior inheritance and/or biological endowment, leaving some members of the 99% in a state of *disillusionment*.

Next Destination

A caregiver's failure to form a bond of love and trust with his or her child shapes an adult who looks to the accumulation of possessions and the approval of others to fill this endless void.

Syed Arshad Husain, M.D. & A. Darius Husain

5

Self-Focus and the Challenges of the Discontented

Rule of the Road: Looking for security? It's in the attachment.

Mile Markers: Attachment, Self-Esteem, Self-Focus, Bullying, Celebrity Worship, Real vs. Ideal Self, Social Comparison, Keeping Up with the Joneses, Eating Disorders, Rosebud

Four former high school chums, George, James, Phil, and Tom, meet for a highly anticipated reunion with their coach to celebrate past victories and relive previous triumphs. Sounds like a scene from any of a myriad of communities across the landscape of the United States. It is also the premise for Jason Miller's play, That Championship Season, winner of Pulitzer and Tony awards. Originally debuting in 1972, the play was a rebuke of time-honored traditions and a challenge to many of the collective values held by society at large.

Set in the coal mining town of Scranton, Pennsylvania, four star athletes return to the house of their former coach to share the last glimmers of glory gleaned from a state basketball championship won 20 years earlier. Like the eroding town in which they grew up, their best days are seemingly behind them. Their once sculpted bodies have given way to the largesse of middle age. Pre-ordained for success, each character is experiencing a career moratorium. One is a weak-principled mayor, another a business-man who has made his living by unsavory wheeling and dealing, and a third, despite being a junior high principal, has contributed little to the young lives he oversees. This lack of movement pales in comparison to the fourth member of the former team whose life ambition is seemingly to drink himself to death. Each of the men have turned to self-destructive behavior—sex, alcohol, criminal endeavors—to fill a void that has steadily grown since that fateful day when they were anointed kings.

The play is a metaphysical lament on missed opportunities, journeys gone astray, and the pitfalls of "winning at all costs." At the center of play stands the coach of these once prominent young men. The most unwilling to look in the mirror and face failure, he is also unable to accept his own mortality as he rapidly approaches death. It was he who instilled the phi-losophy of false superiority, taking shortcuts to achieve perceived great-ness, and engaging in excess when victory had been obtained. Any admit-tance of guilt or remorse for promoting this line of thinking would mean an admission that his entire life and what he stood for was a waste.

While That Championship Season is a fictitious story, its ideas and themes run parallel to the man who brought it to life. Jason Miller, the playwright, was also an outstanding basketball player for his high school in Scranton. The character of Tom, a fledgling author, is loosely based on Miller's life. Like Tom, Miller would endure his own version of peaking early and never experiencing the same level of success. In 1973, the same year he earned accolades for only the second play he had ever written, Mr. Miller won the starring role in the film The Exorcist. His portrayal of Fa-ther Damien Karras earned him an Academy Award nomination. Remark-ably, this performance was his first as an actor in a motion picture. Miller would continue writing and acting for 30 more years but never regain the magic from this wondrous year.

In 2011, his play enjoyed a high profile Broadway revival starring Kiefer Sutherland and Christopher Noth. In an interesting twist, Miller's son Jason Patric took on the role of Tom. In an interview, CBS Sunday Morning narrator Jim Axelrod can't help but notice the parallels between Miller's life and that of his characters. During this same segment, he tours the town of Scranton with Mr. Patric. The son of Mr. Miller acknowledges the significance of resurrecting the play that made his father's career and alludes to perhaps reinvigorating his father's legacy. "I hope this inspires other people, this idea that this kid from this coal mining town went on to do these things in the world of art, literature, and love."

We don't have to be award-winning playwrights and actors, however, to have experienced the central themes of Miller's play. How many of us have attended our own school reunion only to be stunned by the fact that the most popular and celebrated individuals growing up have oftentimes fallen spectacularly from the lofty perches they once occupied? The path to all the treasures of the earth seemingly lay in front of them, yet they wade in a pool of mediocrity. In fact, this scenario has happened so frequently that it has become cliché. Dozens of television shows, movies, and books have harkened high school popularity as the death knell for future success. For the characters in That Championship Season and for many of our fellow human beings, the pinnacle of life occurred when they were 18, and it has been a steep and painful decline ever since.

In the preceding chapter, we discussed how the inability to accept one's biological endowments, an underdeveloped self-concept, and unrealistic expectations can play a role in a life lived unfulfilled. One lesson of value in examining people like George, James, Phil, and Tom or the popularity prince and princesses at our local school revolves around why some people continue to grow and make the necessary adjustments for a healthy life while others are never able to make that leap. Instead, they settle for lives dictated by egocentric pursuits and empty results. While a singular answer for this question is nonexistent, there are benchmarks in development that serve as strong predictors for one's ability to adjust. Of course, these benchmarks happen early in life. In fact, they begin at birth.

From our first breath, infants have tremendous self-focus, a natural drive designed for continued existence, marked by a singular concentration on one's own needs and combined with the hope that a caregiver will ensure these needs are adequately addressed. According to University of Cambridge Professor of Zoology Robert A. Hinde, our "rooting and sucking, clinging, following, [and] crying ... have the biological function of maintaining physical contact, or later, proximity, with the mother."[23] Because the mother is the first source of all that her baby needs—attention, affection, and food, maintaining closeness to her is the object of all her baby's actions. Research shows that the mother-child bond is set in motion before birth and is solidified in the months that follow.

---

23   Bowlby J. The nature of the child's tie to his mother. *International Journal of Psycho-Analysis* 1958; 39:350–373.

In a previous book[24], I wrote about John Bowlby and Mary Ainsworth, behavioral science pioneers who theorized and proved their ideas about how babies depend on a relationship with their caregivers in order to develop socially and emotionally. They believed "that infants are born with a predisposition to behave in ways that will maintain a certain [nearness] and contact with their caregiver" and "that attachment develops as a result of reciprocal caregiver responsiveness to infants' cues." When a mother is attentive and responds positively to the crying, shrieks, babbling, smiling, and gestures her baby uses in order to maintain close connection, the baby develops a trusting view of the mother. His or her attention-seeking behaviors prompt her responsiveness to meeting the baby's needs.

With the mother assuming the roles of provider, protector, and teacher, a natural bond is formed with the child designed to promote survival in the early, helpless days of infancy. This bond creates a secure base from which young children can explore the world and lays the groundwork for further maturity.[25] It keeps children in the proximity of mothers for safety and away from potential predators. Perhaps most important, it helps the child generalize the skill of trust as (s)he moves from trusting Mother, to trusting others, to trusting himself or herself. When this bond is in place, it is what professionals in the behavioral sciences call a "secure attachment." Secure attachment is important because the security the child has with the mother leads to additional feelings of security within the child, which in turn allow the child to formulate self-esteem and self-acceptance.

The reverse is also true. When a child lacks a secure relationship with the mother, feelings of insecurity develop within the child, leading him or her to develop poor self-esteem and self-loathing. Though he may survive infancy, he won't readily explore the outside world, or develop trust in others or himself. Because his caregiver is not trustworthy or responsive, he may develop a false appraisal of himself as unlovable or faulty. He cannot identify his own strengths and believes strongly in a shameful view of himself. This results in poor self-esteem, in which people believe and feel that they are worth little or nothing.

---

24   Husain SA, Cantwell DP. *Fundamentals of Child and Adolescent Psychopathology.* Washington, DC: American Psychiatric Press, 1991.

25   When I speak of "mother" in this chapter, I use the term as shorthand for primary caregiver. The mother figure has rapidly evolved to include father, grandparent, other family member, and adopted parent, to name a few. Despite this variety, two facts remain: 1) The primary caregiver overwhelmingly is still the biological mother; and 2) One singular individual is almost always responsible for establishing secure attachment in infancy.

When a comedian or entertainer attempts to parody a psychiatrist or psychologist, they are likely to conjure up their best German accent and mutter the phrase, "Tell me about your mother." No doubt this line is good for a laugh, but hopefully you are beginning to see how the answer to this statement can uncover a treasure trove of material critical to diagnosis and treatment. This fact becomes even more salient when we compare the attributes of a securely attached child with those of a less secure child.

By the end of early childhood, the securely attached child can access the resources to meet his needs with a great measure of sophistication compared to the helplessness of only a few years before. Development of language, mobility, and coordination helps him or her interact with others and handle daily routines for survival. Trusting relationships that have developed between the child and his/her loved ones and caregivers supply the child with encouragement, belonging, and safety. Thus, self-focus and attention-seeking begin to give way to learning to live in harmony with others, recognizing the importance of others' needs and expectations, and containing his or her own selfish impulses.

However, the child whose attachment is insecure or nonexistent due to abuse or neglect of loved ones and caregivers or from the harshness and trauma of life circumstances (s)he has faced gets stuck in a childish stage of self-focus and attention-seeking. For instance, if a child cannot count on love, trust, or safety in his or her closest relationships, or if his or her new skills of language, mobility, and coordination have no impact on meeting the child's basic needs of food, shelter, and clothing, the child will often fall back on infant mechanisms for survival, looking for the attention of others—any others—to meet his or her needs for emotional security. The poor self-esteem that develops from his or her unmet needs and unreliable relationship with his or her caregiver leaves him or her with a persistent self-focus that has negative consequences for adolescent and adult life.

One high profile byproduct of this insecure attachment and persistent self-focus, receiving added attention and scrutiny on both television airwaves and school board meetings alike, is the issue of bullying. Before diving too far into this topic, it is important to distinguish between bullying and other behaviors that are exhibited as part of the natural developmental process. Because one child pushes another to the ground or calls another child an unflattering name does not necessarily make the first child a bully. In most cases, these actions are situational and are a result of children attempting to understand and navigate their environment. With proper guidance from adults, children learn to express themselves in more appropriate and socially acceptable fashion. Bullying, on the other hand, is defined by The American Academy of Child and Adolescent Psychiatry as "repeated negative acts by one or more children against another child." The bullying behavior may involve verbal harassment, physical assault, or coercion, and may have a racial, religious, or sexual overtone. Bullying is frequently reported by children and adolescents in and around a school setting and may include physical and verbal threats.

There are many factors as to why a child or adolescent engages in the act of bullying and no single formula can lead to an exact answer for how this damaging behavior develops in a youth. There are, however, several common risk factors that increase the odds of a child becoming a "bully." They include witnessing abusive behavior in the home as a means of problem solving, a general need to achieve and assert control, difficulty managing and expressing emotions, and desire to receive attention. All of these characteristics are more likely to contribute to or manifest from a caregiver-child insecure attachment. Research also shows that the number one way to reduce the likelihood of a boy or girl engaging in bullying tendencies is to instill in them a sense of empathy for other children. The first opportunity to promote empathy also occurs in the early mother and infant interactions. Thus, the insecure attachment is a double-edged sword: It increases the chances for an environment that fosters bullying, and it reduces the probability that one will be exposed to the antidote.

Bullying and an individual's attempt to escape this torment is by no means a new concept. It has been the subject of stories told and untold for centuries. The title character from Cinderella, a tale that has over 700 versions spread across all societies of the world, is wickedly bullied by her stepsisters. Only through magic, her beautiful appearance, and the resources of a powerful prince is she able to remove herself from this tragic state.[26] While the idea of bullying is nothing original, it has attracted significant public attention lately because of the negative and at times tragic outcomes leading to suicide or the retaliatory acts of violence against the alleged bullies. For example, Grammy Award nominated hit, "Pumped Up Kicks" (downloaded over four million times and dubbed the official anthem of the summer of 2011 by multiple musical media outlets) by Foster the People is about a kid who is bullied by his peers to the point where he finds a gun and shoots them.

---

26   This recipe sounds remarkably similar to the three most common ways a person achieves traditional power, identified in Chapter 2: uncanny luck (fairy godmother), genetic advantages (natural good looks), and inherited wealth (the prince).

Much of the modern focus of bullying revolves around the more sophisticated and effective tools available to the perpetrator. Whereas bullies were not so long ago required to be in the presence of their victims, the wide reach of the Internet and social media have allowed the ridicule and hate to continue 24 hours a day. In addition, an unflattering comment, picture, or video regarding the person being harassed can be sent instantaneously to large numbers of people. Those best in a position to keep a watchful eye and intercede when necessary are often handcuffed because of the vast nature of these forums and one's ability to interact with them anonymously. At an age when reputation and obtaining the positive opinion of one's peers can take on an obsessive quality, the ability to exploit an adolescent's weakness or perceived flaw has increased exponentially in a few short years. This development has led to some horrific news headlines in otherwise "quiet communities."

Fortunately, we have reached a watershed moment in our viewpoint of bullying. No longer are these actions considered a natural part of growing up. People are beginning to realize the detrimental impact of these behaviors as evident by the onslaught of anti-bullying legislation and public service campaigns. This outcry is an important advance for the consequences to those being bullied and even those who engage in the bullying can no longer be ignored. Thus, it is paramount that we provide adequate education and the necessary resources to assist both the bullied and bully alike. Part of that education includes the examination of insecure attachment and the resulting poor self-esteem and self-focus.

Bullying is not the only negative outcome associated with the side effects of an insecure attachment. Projection is an ego protective defense mechanism in which we take our own negative characteristics, feelings, or thoughts and pretend that they really belong to other people around us. For example, if I realize that I have feelings of greed and jealousy about someone else's possessions or good fortune, I dump those feelings onto the people around me, pretending that they are jealous of me and want what I have. While projection provides a measure of mental and emotional relief as we dump our burdens on others, it also demands the upkeep of a false self and a constant distrust of others. These tasks are wearying and destructive, but many ordinary people, beleaguered by the self-focus that persists after childhood abuse, trauma, or poor attachment, find themselves regularly engaged in doing them. This approach leads to a generalized discomfort of discontent. In our quest to rid ourselves of these feelings, we try to one-up those around us to achieve superiority or identify with a powerful figure by imitating his or her persona in as many ways as we can.

George, James, Tom, and Phil all project a sense of accomplishment when the true feelings of inadequacy and discontent are actually present and, while the childhoods of the four former standout athletes are barely chronicled in That Championship Season, would it be a surprise if it were determined that these characters had complicated relationships with their primary caregivers that led to poor attachment? All have adopted a style of one-upmanship that has proved to be destructive. Each gravitates to a power figure in the coach and imitates his "lessons" and values throughout their lives. In the end, the four have extreme difficulties in forming and maintaining lasting, meaningful relationships.

Unfortunately for George, James, Tom, and Phil, they grew up in the much more reserved decade of the 1950s. Otherwise, they would be excellent candidates to be treated by one of the numerous pop psychologists occupying the airwaves. Actor-comedian Jim Gaffigan, who played the role of George in the 2011 version of That Championship Season, states, "To me, this is about men, real men, in a pre-Dr. Phil era."

Too bad, because one of the more recognizable of these television self-help gurus, Dr. Drew Pinsky, has mastered the combination of technically sound treatment theory and approach with a population of insecure, high profile adults who covet the limelight. His practice, viewed by millions of people on such shows as Celebrity Rehab and Sober House is paradoxical in nature: The very reason many of these individuals are willing to be treated in front of the public eye is emblematic of the insecurities and resulting narcissism that help fuel their addictions.

While Dr. Drew has many advocates and fans as well as critics and detractors, one thing is for certain: He is spot on with his appreciation for the consequences of a child who develops an insecure attachment. He writes, "Children in such circumstances tend to misinterpret or disregard feelings, suffer from an inability to connect with others, and find it difficult to regulate their emotions." He goes on to say that such a child can become an adult who is "... haunted by chronic feelings of loneliness, emptiness, and self-loathing and seeks to replace that disconnection with a sense of worth and importance fueled by others."

For celebrities and non-celebrities suffering from poor self-esteem, the individual creates a false self that places beliefs about personal inadequacies on the back burner. The false self we project when we feel inadequate is made up of attributes, mannerisms, and a personal style that we believe to be ideal. Our adoption of these ideal attributes, mannerisms, and personal style choices is designed, according to Pinsky, "to prime that continual stream of admiration and desire" from others—positive attention we crave in order to cope with our deep insecurity.

According to Sam Vaknin, Ph.D., who has written widely on the topic of narcissism, "any kind of attention is usually deemed ... to be preferable to obscurity."[27] He notes that "notoriety and infamy" alike fuel the empty tanks of those trying to navigate life with poor self-esteem.

The nature of modern celebrity attracts those seeking affirmation outside themselves or those who immediately surround them. Indeed, the celebrities engaged in therapy with Dr. Drew outwardly seem confident, content, and living a dream, especially when their status with the public is at its epicenter. When the roar of the crowd begins to fade or inevitably fails to cover up underlying issues of inferiority, these individuals will often turn to alcohol, drugs, and other risky behaviors in an attempt to fill a canyon of poor self-esteem. Miller astutely understood this concept and portrayed his characters as unraveled once the reasons for their relative celebrity status were no longer perpetuated by the cheers and hero worship of their small community. Likewise, the popular kids in high school may experience a rude awakening once the qualities that allowed their inflated significance are deemed superficial in the adult world.

Ironically, those suffering from insecurity look to these celebrities both locally and globally as models for a satisfying life when in reality many suffer from the same ailments as those who idolize them. This dynamic is one of the more powerful ones in perpetuating our society's celebrity infatuation. At the heart of this infatuation is the status and access to life's riches that accompany celebrity. We compare what we have and how we live to those who constantly bask in the limelight, and we realize that we have the short end of the stick. Regardless of whether or not we participate in celebrity worship, most of us (possibly all of us) are guilty of comparing ourselves if not with celebrities then with the people around us. Nothing seems to make us feel more momentarily secure or permanently anxious about ourselves than comparing ourselves to others.

The theory of social comparison, developed in 1954 by American social psychologist Leon Festinger,[28] rests on a belief that people want to

---

27   Vaknin S. *Malignant Self-Love. Narcissism Revisited. Narcissistic and Psychopathic Leaders.* Prague: Narcissus Publications, 1999; p. 37. Retrieved October 30, 2014 from http://www.narcissistic-abuse.com/narcissistleader.pdf

28   Festinger L. A Theory of Social Comparison Processes. *Human Relations* 1954; 7:117–140.

have an accurate view of their abilities and opinions, and thus we compare ourselves with others as a means of personal evaluation. Festinger thought it was important that we measure ourselves against people who are similar to us so we can understand how people with the same resources and backgrounds fare at the personal challenges we may attempt. Upward social comparisons show our interest in improving as we measure ourselves against individuals or groups who are more advanced or established in various areas. To make ourselves feel better, we at times engage in making downward social comparisons, which highlight our accomplishments as we compare ourselves to individuals or groups who are less advanced and established. Used correctly, social comparison might give us an accurate marker of our progress toward some well-defined goal or skill and allow us to feel the corresponding inspiration or pride. Unfortunately, we often don't use it that way.

Already wounded by poor self-esteem and looking outward for affirmation of their own worth, people with persistent self-focus use social comparison to further inflate their ideal self—their "cover" for the real self of whom they are ashamed. Upward comparison makes them feel inferior and depressed, but it also gives them observable characteristics to aspire to in projecting their false self. Downward comparison makes self-focused people feel superior to others, but it also creates fear surrounding their own inferiority compared to those with higher status and more resources than the self-focused people themselves have. In short, comparing ourselves to others always upsets our contentment with what we have. It makes us question the adequacy of what we possess and ultimately places our contentment outside of our own control.

Remember, self-focused adults are looking to others to affirm their worth. They display attention-seeking behaviors in order to prompt the attention, affection, and care that they did not receive as children. They are strongly motivated to mask their feelings of inadequacy with achievements, possessions, and desirability. In a culture where they can be sold the tools to succeed at these efforts, it is easy for them to get trapped in a cycle of comparing themselves with others and keeping up appearances.

Cartoonist Arthur "Pop" Momand saw people like this left and right in his Cedarhurst, New York neighborhood in the early 1900s and developed what the New York Times called "a comic strip parody of American domestic life." The strip Keeping Up with the Joneses was about the McGinnis family, who envied their well-to-do neighbors and tried to live up to their classy standards. The strip's title is a phrase that has been incorporated into the modern vernacular. The phrase can be found in multiple entertainment mediums (there is a 2009 movie centering on the concept called The Joneses) and is referenced in multiple articles and publications centering on such diverse topics as business investing, health care, and education.

Various research studies have also examined the "Joneses Effect" on individual belief and behavior. One of the more classic studies involves two scenarios from which participants in the experiment must choose. In the first scenario, you make a comfortable salary of $100,000 but everyone you associate with earns $120,000. For the second, you draw a lesser yearly sum of $50,000; however, your peers make only $30,000. In each case, the cost of buying goods—whether a house, car, or milk—is the same. With the former, you have much more purchasing power, but you must live with the knowledge that you are at the bottom of the earnings totem pole. With the latter, you have only half the resources, but you can be comforted by the fact that you have more than everyone else around you. Remarkably, the vast majority of individuals preferred to be perceived as "top dog" at the expense of earning more money and having more financial security.

A similar study conducted by Michael Harris, Frederik Anseel, and Filip Lievens published in the *Journal of Applied Psychology*[29] examines the relationship between salary comparison and levels of pay satisfaction. What they discovered is that individuals were more likely to be content with their salary if it compared favorably to those doing similar work. This finding is certainly not revolutionary until you factor in that this variable was a greater predictor of salary satisfaction then the total amount an individual earned. In essence, a person doing work for $35,000 that normally pays $25,000 is likely to be happier with their compensation than someone who earns $75,000 doing work that normally warrants $85,000.

These bodies of research illustrate the considerable influence of social comparison. Even among those who haven't experienced childhood abuse, trauma, or attachment problems, making comparisons can easily lead a person to feel that his or her "differences" from others are personal "inadequacies" that (s)he must hide or diminish. Our discontent with our real self by comparison leads us to try to self-improve according to the latest fad or ad and compete with others to prove our superiority. However, our desire for more creates a liability for us. It can cause us to lack concern for others and lose confidence that we can access the resources necessary

---

29   Harris MM, Anseel F, Lievens F. Keeping Up With the Joneses: A Field Study of the Relationships among Upward, Lateral, and Downward Comparisons and Pay Level Satisfaction. *Journal of Applied Psychology* 2008; 93(3):665–673.

to meet our real needs. At its worst, we may find ourselves purposefully trampling the rights of others and disregarding morality and acceptable social behavior because of our extreme self-focus. This has helped lead to increased accounts of adult bullying in family structures, neighborhoods, and work places. In a study focusing on employees in the United States, over 40% stated they have experienced verbal and/or psychological abuse at their jobs and 13% claim that this abuse occurs weekly.

Part of the prevalence of adult bullying stems from our belief that our own worth lies in our possession of the unobtainable ideal. In turn, this ideal creates a discontent with actual reality that is hard to escape. The discontent leads us to strive for different circumstances, and the comparisons that identify what is ideal only make us feel more ashamed of who we are and lead us into deeper conflict with those around us. Too often in today's culture of ever-increasing needs and sense of entitlement, we pursue power, security, approval, convenience, and happiness with one goal: "Look out for number one." In such an environment, our fellow man is our competitor; his success, a source of our contempt; his failures, a source of our judgment; his way of life, a threat to ours. Believing in our entitlement, yet lacking possession of those things to which we feel entitled, we look outward, comparing ourselves to others and competing against them in order to obtain power and contentment for ourselves.

The majority of people have desires, fantasies, goals, hopes, and dreams. Our ideal self is the person we assume we will be when such visions are finally accomplished. We put all of our hopes for contentment into the basket of our ideal self, believing that when we reach our ideal, then we will be happy, then we will have peace, then we will cease suffering. However, we dispute the very definition of contentment—satisfaction with our current circumstance—with our striving for more than what we have and are. When a person cares about being accepted, envied, or praised, if they don't get the response they want from others, they, too, become discontent. People have been led to believe that having titles, money, and possessions will make them feel good, but often when they get them, they don't feel content because other people have still more than what exists in their ledger. This leads to a permanent feeling of not owning enough. This is a belief that, while false, wreaks havoc on people's ability to feel contentment and even leads them to commit desperate acts in order to obtain truly nonessential stuff.

The desperate acts become more complicated when brewed under conditions of celebrity worship promulgated in modern society. The 24 hour access to their seemingly glamorous lives sets the stage for an impossible social comparison. Ultimately, it can create a mismatch between our ideal selves and our real selves.

One of the most visible and devastating examples of the consequences of this mismatch is the epidemic of eating disorders in the United States. According to the National Eating Disorders Association (NEDA), more than 20 million women and 10 million men in America suffer from eating disorders.[30] The most common eating disorders are anorexia, characterized by calorie restriction by limited eating and/or excessive exercise, and bulimia, characterized by a binge and purge cycle. While girls and young women are most likely to suffer from these disorders, boys and young men are increasingly vulnerable. NEDA reports that boys and girls as young as seven years old have been diagnosed with an eating disorder; it is currently the third most prevalent chronic disease among adolescents. This phenomenon is not purely American in nature, however; eating disorders are becoming more of a health crisis in many industrialized nations, including Japan.

The reason for the onset of eating disorders is complicated and varied. There are elements of anxiety, depression, and even obsessive compulsive disorder that can accompany an eating disorder. It would be misleading to pinpoint one cause for such a diverse disorder; however, anorexia and bulimia are often associated with a pathological thinking that a person's body is not right or normal because it differs from that of peers, older women, or celebrities and models considered to be ideal. NEDA estimates that "35–57% of adolescent girls engage in crash dieting, fasting, self-induced vomiting, diet pills, or laxatives." One of the major issues is that obtaining an ideal weight is not enough to bring satisfaction to people suffering from these disorders (especially anorexia). They often surpass any designated weight loss goal and begin to enter a level of emaciation that can seriously affect core body functioning and even lead to death. NEDA reports that anorexia nervosa has the highest mortality rate of any psychiatric disorder.

Eating disorders can be an extremely tangible example of the dangers of a comparative culture where the real self and the ideal self comes into conflict. A person with anorexia literally is wasting away before our eyes. However, those without an eating disorder can have an equally dangerous and more gradual form of erosion that takes hold in the mind, body, and soul. When we allow our self-focus to take over, our ideal self becomes

---

30   National Eating Disorders Association. Get the Facts on Eating Disorders. Retrieved October 30, 2014 from https://www.nationaleatingdisorders.org/get-facts-eating-disorders

so elevated that our real self will never match it. This imbalance can be demoralizing, seemingly inescapable, and even traumatic. People work impressively hard to resolve this imbalance, but self-focus, which fuels that pursuit, conversely refuses to allow us freedom from our strife.

At whatever life station or social status we find ourselves, "better" possessions, "better" circumstances, and "better" status promise the security, confidence, and fulfillment that we all hope to experience in life. However, this thinking has the potential to lead to great desire and discontent. If we want what's "better," our desires will never be satisfied for there is always something "better." Perhaps we want a new model car or a vacation home to add to the collection of status tokens, or we work nonstop past retirement age to increase our potential pension just a little bit more. Regardless of the aim, we risk believing that "strong wants" are "needs" and invest time, effort, and money into prioritizing them as though they were the latter. Suddenly, we find ourselves unable to tolerate less than what we have become accustomed to having or have hoped to gain. Unable to tolerate less, we become slaves to various means of producing more—be they violence, overwork, debt, stealing, exploitation, or dishonesty.

While there is nothing wrong with planning for future needs or a big-ticket purchase, ill-defined pursuits of "better" outcomes typically don't result in the provision and pleasure we hope they will. Comparing ourselves with someone else's situation rather than being content with what we have and who we are is the basis of our desire for "better." The word is comparative by nature, requiring people to focus their attention outside of themselves, desiring more than what other people have in order to affirm their own positions as powerful and high-status. Having more—which we pay for dearly and repeatedly—promises power but produces vulnerability as we commit ourselves to debt, overwork, and worry trying to mimic someone else's lifestyle and show ourselves superior to others. When we are inclined to want more, we have shackled ourselves, forever chained to the insatiable beast that is the ideal self.

That is how I found myself, a physician and medical director, less powerful than a social worker who made one-sixth of my income. In my mind, I had created an image of what a person in my position should own and possesses: a large house, a luxury car, fine clothing. This pursuit of a false ideal restricted me from making the same choices as my friend and colleague, Bob. I fell into this trap despite my emotionally satisfying upbringing and secure attachment. Those less fortunate, with an insecure attachment and childhood unfulfilled, face an even greater uphill battle.

Every time I revisit the importance of self-focus and secure attachment, I am reminded of one of my first exposures to American culture, the film classic Citizen Kane. I was very young at the time and did not possess the psychological background to completely appreciate all the themes and nuances. Like many who have viewed the film over the years (the American Film Institute lists it as the greatest movie of all time), I enjoyed the story, dramatic conflict, and sheer scope of this masterpiece. After additional exposure later in the life, I realized that this icon of American cinema is the perfect illustration of the perils of an insecure attachment.

The film opens with media titan Charles Kane lying on his deathbed. Despite being wealthy beyond anyone's wildest desires, he is dying alone, a broken man. With his last breath, he shouts, "Rosebud!" The rest of the movie focuses on two interwoven plot threads: 1) the rise to power of Charles Kane, and 2) a reporter's attempt to understand the significance of "Rosebud." The audience learns that Kane uses his considerable resources to manipulate wars, elections, and his close relationships. He is the personification of a bully, participating in numerous inexcusable acts and showing little remorse for the lives he damages. The audience also learns that Kane's childhood was filled with pain and sorrow. His parents are initially poor until an act of sheer luck dramatically changes their fortunes. Despite this newfound status (or because of it), a young Kane is purposely separated from his mother and raised by an appointed guardian an entire coast away.

The reporter never discovers the true meaning of the word "rosebud." However, those willing to sit through this epic movie are rewarded with the answer: Rosebud is the name of the sled from his youth. A man of numerous, costly possessions, the one most meaningful was symbolic of the childhood he once had and then lost.

Kane is the archetype of the insecure child. Scared by the abandonment of those trusted to care for him, Kane attempts to regain the power he lost by projecting an image of superiority and invincibility. Filled with mistrust, he is unable to forge any lasting relationship and treats people like assets to be spent and discarded at his whim.

Orson Welles, the multitalented director, writer, and actor in the film, was a master of psychology. He was, after all, the man who convinced members of his War of the Worlds radio audience that an alien invasion was occurring. Welles certainly understood the perils of a traumatic childhood and how individuals overcompensate for their shortcomings. Indeed, most critics conclude that Welles was modeling the character of Kane after newspaper mogul William Randolph Hearst. Welles wanted to emphasize that the powerful are often driven by a compulsion resulting from an unsatisfied childhood need. Hearst was no exception. His fame and fortune masked a life filled with adultery and bigotry. This destructive behavior helped sow the seeds of near financial ruin.

Kane, his inspiration Hearst, and Miller's characters from That Championship Season are reminders to us all that the contemporary measures of power, including prestige, money, and material goods, will never be a substitute for the feeling of being authentically loved and cared for by those most important to us. Whether with real people or fictional characters based on reality, the importance of a secure attachment and accompanying positive sense of self is evident. For in the end, we all desire our own personal "rosebud."

Power Points

- A *secure attachment*, developed when the primary caregiver is able to meet the needs of a child, is essential for formulating self-esteem and self-acceptance.

- Children with an *insecure attachment* often have feelings of inadequacy and enhanced self-focus that increase the likelihood of antisocial behaviors such as bullying.

- As adults, the insecurely attached have a large gap between their *real self* and *ideal self*, leading to the likelihood of seeking out material possessions and the approval of others in a futile and often destructive attempt to achieve life satisfaction.

- Regardless of our *attachment style,* we are all vulnerable to *social comparison* that creates an endless and costly cycle of trying to "keep up" with our peers in the types of clothes we wear, the cars we drive, and the homes we live in.

- Even the rich and powerful find *disillusionment* in the quest for the possessions they have attained and return to what we are all looking for: meaningful relationships with those we most care about.

Next Destination

In Chapter 6, we will examine how the media has become a powerful tool that allows the elite to capitalize on the consumer's feelings of inadequacy and need to socially compare.

Syed Arshad Husain, M.D. & A. Darius Husain

6

And Now a Word from Our Sponsors

Rule of the Road: Chances are you're happy
(despite the best efforts of the media).

Mile Markers: Happiness, Life Evaluation, Media, Consumer, Arab Spring, Mad Men, Marketing to the Vulnerable, Portable Status Symbols, The Mortgage Crisis, Product Placement, Media Planning, Internet Profiling, RFID Chips

Next time you're sitting around with friends and looking for a way to spice up the dinner table conversation, try asking this question: What income level does someone have to reach that making any more money is unlikely to increase their happiness? Now, some will outright reject the entire nature of the question. More dollars, they will argue, obviously means more happiness. A group of intelligent people from Princeton University would beg to differ, however, as their data has established an income/happiness threshold. Once achieved, a member of the 99% is likely to experience as much happiness as your run-of-the-mill multimillionaire with a home in the Hamptons.

The entertaining part about asking this question is not only what the group will guess to be the threshold, but how they go about determining their response. There will be those who will throw an answer out right away. Most likely, these individuals are prone to impulsive, jump-first-and-ask-questions-later behaviors in other aspects of their lives. They are probably fun to spend a night out on the town with, yet you'd get nervous if they started dating your daughter. Others will ask a series of questions in order to narrow down a plausible answer. Typical clarifications include: Is this individual single, or does he or she have a family? How many people in the family? What part of the country is this person from? Does this person live in the big city or in a more rural area?

Thankfully, the Princeton researchers' mammoth sample size of 450,000 limits the impact of these variables and inspires confidence that their number plays well in many scenarios and parts of the country, including Peoria. Once all questions have been answered to the satisfaction of your audience, then the guessing can begin. You will come across the occasional avid Trivial Pursuit player who shouts out a lowball response (conditioned to believe why ask a question if it has an obvious answer). In almost every instance, however, people often overestimate the threshold by hundreds of thousands if not millions of dollars.

Now that all of the information has been presented, I will give you a chance to weigh in. To give you enough time, I will reveal it to you in the style of the great boardwalk hustlers and infomercial promoters. According to the Princeton researchers, who by the way are a part of the 1% of the biologically endowed for intelligence, the threshold is neither $1,000,000 nor $500,000. It's not $400,000, $300,000, nor even $200,000. Can you believe this most coveted gift can be yours for under $100,000? In fact, today $75,000 is all you need to experience everyday happiness on the same level as many of the CEOs of the Fortune 500. This $75,000 can be paid to you in 24 equal payments of $3,125. Operators are standing by.

What is so magical about $75,000? The researchers suggest, "Perhaps $75,000 is a threshold beyond which further increases in income no longer improve individuals' ability to do what matters most to their emotional well-being, such as spending time with people they like, avoiding pain and disease, and enjoying leisure. "[31] They go on to state that, "It also is likely that when income rises beyond this value, the increased ability to purchase positive experiences is balanced, on average, by some negative effects."

Let's examine both ends of this equation. Individuals and families making less than $75,000 are more likely to report high levels of stress. In fact, stress increases as income steadily declines from $75,000. In these sce-

---

31   Kahneman D, Deaton A. High income improves evaluation of life but not emotional well-being. *Proceedings of the National Academy of Sciences* 2010; 107(38): 16489–16493.

narios, people start worrying about the ability to provide basic necessities for themselves and their loved ones such as food, clothing, and shelter. A person worried about where and when he or she will obtain the next meal is unlikely to indulge in the pleasures of a chess game with the neighbor. Instead, daily life is preoccupied by staying afloat and, in many cases, core survival. For those on the opposite end of the spectrum, the additional income is often accompanied by additional stress for different reasons. This reality can include longer hours at work, increased responsibility and scrutiny, and less time to enjoy the fruits of their labor.

For you astute readers, these findings seemingly contradict the research presented in the previous chapter. The conclusions of both the "Joneses Effect" and the "Pay Satisfaction" research indicate that people engage in frequent social comparison and have a higher level of satisfaction if their income is favorable to their peers. Practically speaking, it would not be the first time that results of two independent studies contradict each other. However, careful review of the Princeton study accounts for this presumed disparity. One can boil it down to the difference in two subdivisions of happiness: emotional well-being versus life evaluation. Emotional well-being centers more on how we are feeling on a particular day. Is a person reporting joy, pleasure, and wonder, or sadness, guilt, and frustration? It is in this category that there exists little distinction between the average person making $75,000 and the average person making $1,000,000. In contrast, life evaluation is more concerned with how an individual would rate the direction their life is going. In other words, emotional well-being is an immediate snapshot of how one is feeling in the moment whereas life evaluation takes a step back and asks the same individual if he or she is advancing in the world as hoped and dreamed.

In life evaluation, the $75,000 threshold no longer is relevant. In general, the more income a person generates, the more likely are increased positive life evaluations. Greater income allows individuals to believe they have achieved a higher status and affords them greater access to goods, services, and experiences. This correlates nicely with the findings in the Keeping up with the Joneses and Pay Satisfaction studies. It also is an astounding conclusion: Two people may experience the exact same feelings of happiness each day and yet have very different perceptions about the direction in which their lives are going. In addition, the dissimilarities in their life evaluations can be attributed almost entirely to their disparity in income.

The reasons for this phenomenon can be varied. Recall our previous discussion on self vs. ideal self. Many individuals with an insecure attachment have a large gap between how they see themselves (self) and who they wish they could be (ideal self). When asked to evaluate their lives, these same people often offer a negative outlook because of a fixation on an unobtainable outcome. They can never reach the heights of their fabricated ideal and even if they do, it does little to alleviate their dissatisfaction. The subsequent feelings are often depression and oppression resulting in self-destructive behavior.

Even individuals with secure attachments who have the ability to foster meaningful relationships, achieve emotional stability, and navigate in their environment with a positive outlook struggle to achieve a baseline of general satisfaction. These are the same people who view themselves as happy and have a pretty healthy ratio of daily ups versus downs. Still, their life evaluations are lower than those they deem to have a greater piece of the pie. It is almost as if they are saying, "I am happy, but I would feel better about the direction of my life if I had a little bit more."

I hope it is fairly simple to see the futility of this line of thinking. Even if this "little bit more" is achieved, it only fuels the desire to reach the next incremental level. There is no stopping this feedback loop because there are infinite levels of a "little bit more," and there will always be someone who will have "a little bit more" than you. Still, nearly every human being walking this planet struggles with putting the brakes on this cycle.

Much of this challenge can be attributed to the fact that we are all inundated with information about who we are supposed to be and what we are supposed to have. The moment we turn on the television, browse the Internet, flip through a magazine, check our Facebook news feed, or switch on the radio in our car, we encounter different translations of the same message: What we haven't gained by birth or equal-opportunity mandate is for sale, and all we have to do in order to "be more" is "buy more." A beautiful girl tells us the type of makeup she wears, confiding that she trusts nothing but this particular brand to bring out her natural beauty while it covers flaws like acne blemishes and midday shine. A muscled young man admits that all of his attempts to bulk up had failed until he bought the home gym placed artfully behind him. A sleek luxury SUV stops outside of a nightclub, dispensing a carful of laughing, stylishly-dressed friends, the driver handing the brand-embossed keys to a valet while shooting us a knowing grin. It appears that these people have the beauty, the body, and the relationships we desire. Why not adopt their "tried and true methods" by consuming the products they've used?

The short answer is because little of what we see on screens, tablets, storefronts, billboards, or packaging ever reaches us without the intervention of people—writers, producers, makeup artists, hairstylists, wardrobe designers, lighting designers, set designers, editors, programmers, webmasters, and special effects personnel—who work behind-the-scenes to make the final images we see appear flawless and enticing. Paid models and actors, selected for their faces and physiques, are styled, lighted, and airbrushed to present an ideal image, and deliver expert performances from a script drafted especially to arouse our insecurities and longings. It's their handiwork that makes the wealth, celebrity, and extravagant lifestyles of the elite appear so normal, attractive, and within reach. As a result, ordinary people often become desperate for a life they lack the resources to achieve. They end up searching constantly for a way to fill up the void they feel due to what they perceive as their comparatively lower status. The average channel-surfer would be hard-pressed to unpack such a sophisticated communications ploy in a few seconds of observation, but the impressions conveyed stand to remain all the way with the consumer to the store.

The images we see portrayed and praised in the media are merely tools that create and take advantage of an individual's feelings of inadequacy so that commercial ventures can profit. The life evaluation that we are "not enough" or that we "don't have enough" are universal responses to these powerful visual messages. These messages cause us to turn inward, aware and ashamed of our own lack of resources and desirability, and outward, assuming that the solution for our condition lies beyond ourselves. This inward focus and outward dependence mirrors our natural condition at birth but has problematic consequences in adulthood, including discontent with who we are and what we have.

To categorize the media only as a pariah, however, would be an unfortunate oversimplification as media have been and continue to be put to many socially-responsible and culturally-enriching uses. The Arab Spring of 2011 occurring in Egypt, Syria, Libya, Yemen, and Bahrain illustrated the tremendous power of the Internet and social media tools such as Facebook and Twitter. They contain the ability to link people together and provide them with rapidly changing information at lightning speeds. Average citizens were able to rally in great numbers and with one voice against the oppressive activities of long-entrenched regimes. These leaders, able for decades to hold on to power often at the expense of the people they were supposed to represent, were forced to answer the demands of the populace. This wave of expression swept across the region and began to rede-fine the nature of the conversation between government and the people. In many ways, the Arab Spring was a victory for human rights and com-mon decency. While it would be naïve to believe that the vast corruption and totalitarian behavior of these countries' political systems have been thwarted[32], the initial spark for change would not have been possible with-out modern media infrastructures.

Media's influence can be benevolent, but it is the manner in which it is used to exploit that gives us pause. Today's media glorifies perfection and advances materialism, emphasizing the necessity of an opulence that the world's majority of ordinary people don't have and can't afford. However, television viewers' lack of the biological, positional, and financial trappings for a powerful existence of their own provides an opportunity to sell them a remedy for their disadvantaged lot. Media outlets have a lot to gain by selling their time, space, and viewers to advertisers who desire this already-captive audience. For this reason, scenarios and images of ease, pleasure, influence, and enviable sophistication appear on relatively every media screen and surface we witness. They promulgate a sense of deficiency and want within us and deliver us to advertisers. This form of commercialism, the practice of making everything for sale and every person a potential buyer, has one goal—to manufacture need in human beings so that virtu-ally anything can be sold for profit.

Interestingly enough, our fascination with material possessions even extends to the process of how these products are packaged for the masses. One of the most talked about and critically acclaimed television shows of our time centers around the extraordinary lengths to which advertisers will go to sell their client's products. Mad Men, a show airing on AMC, has won 15 Emmys since its inception in 2007, including the Emmy for outstanding drama in four consecutive years. The series centers on a cut-throat, win-at-all-cost advertising agency in the 1960s. Despite the histori-cal setting, the creators have been lauded for their understanding and ap-preciation of contemporary issues. The central character is the charismatic Don Draper. Ironically, the man, who is as skilled as they come at mer-chandise makeovers, is the byproduct of an extreme alteration himself. We learn that Draper's real name is Dick Whitman, the son of a prostitute; he failed to graduate from high school and had no alternative but to enlist in the Army. While serving in the Korean War, Whitman fortuitously used a tragic accident as a means to swap identities with his commanding officer,

---

32   In places like Egypt, much to the chagrin of that country's 99%, it seems one form of corruption was overthrown only to be replaced by another form of corruption.

a learned gentleman named Don Draper. Because Whitman was keen on the advantages possessed by Draper, he parlayed one man's unfortunate luck to promote his own standing.

Draper (Whitman) embodies his false identity with bravado and charm. What better way for a con man to make his living than to reimagine ordinary products as life-altering elixirs? In the pilot episode, the audience learns both the cunning and callousness of his salesman's techniques during a dinner table conversation with an enticing young woman. When the subject of love is brought up he tells her, "By love you mean big lightning bolts to the heart, where you can't eat and you can't work, and you just run off and get married and make babies. The reason you haven't felt it is because it doesn't exist. What you call love was invented by guys like me to sell nylons."

This oft-quoted line serves as a window into a man whose soul is empty. He is also a metaphor for an entire society whose sense of self-worth is directly connected to goods and services that have no intrinsic value. Don Draper[33] attempts to fill his bottomless void with alcohol, luxuries, and women just as we attempt to address our own misgivings about ourselves with the latest must-have possession. The more he consumes, the more he cheats on his wife, the more he denies his true nature, the further he travels into his own darkness. Watching Draper is like holding up a mirror, albeit with a slightly more attractive reflection, showing that the pursuit of inconsequential things only increases the sensation of being hollow.

After several seasons of the audience getting to know this man, it is unclear if Draper truly believes that some of humanity's most sought-after emotions and intimate experiences are simply manufactured by those controlling the information. Regardless, it is clear he realizes that exploiting our deepest desires is extremely profitable. Under this pretense, every potential threat, problem, and occasion in existence provides a source for a marketing event. On a television show, in the security and privacy of your own home, it makes for riveting, often humorous entertainment. In the real world, where seemingly nothing is sacred or off limits, it becomes more difficult to admire.

This thought is most evident by the fact that these marketing events are targeted to an increasingly vulnerable audience. It is especially difficult to digest when this targeting starts with young children. According to the Media Awareness Network, children "represent an important demo-

---

33 Draper probably would have found good company in William Randolph Hearst and George, James, Tom and Phil from *That Championship Season*. That is of course, if misery truly loves company.

graphic to marketers because they have their own purchasing power, they influence their parents' buying decisions, and they're the adult consumers of the future."[34] To effectively reach children and to ensure their message is most potent, companies are collectively spending billions of kid-centric advertising dollars annually and have gone so far as to hire experts in child development, including child psychologists, to fine-tune their approach.

In many cases, this tactic will have limited consequences, such as increased headaches for parents who constantly have to thwart the insistent pleas of their children while shopping for groceries at Wal-Mart. In other cases, the results can be longer lasting and more detrimental. A staggering 33% of all children in the United States are considered overweight or obese.[35] Since one of the leading predicators of adult obesity is childhood obesity, this finding borders on a national crisis. A study conducted by Nielsen Monitor-Plus/Nielsen Media Research on the advertising exposure of 2- to 11-year-olds sheds some light on some of the causes. Its report suggests that the average child sees 25,600 forms of advertisement on television alone. About 5,500 of these ads are food related.[36] While this category constitutes about 22% of the ads a child witnesses, an additional 43% of advertisements are for a product that promotes sedentary activities such as video games and other television programming.

Researchers Debra Desrochers and Debra Holt[37], who have spent an enormous amount of time mining the data, suggest the combination of these two factors (advertising food and sedentary activity) is what places these children at greater risk for being overweight or obese. It is also important to realize that the 25,600 commercial ad exposures are limited to television, a media that is relatively regulated, and exclude Internet adver-

---

34   Media Awareness Network. How Marketers Target Kids. Retrieved October 30, 2014 from http://www.flagarts.com/faculty-staff/Jennifer%20Spensieri/documents/ HowMarketersTargetKids.doc

35   Centers for Disease Control and Prevention. Adolescent and School Health. Childhood Obesity Facts. Retrieved October 30, 2014 from http://www.cdc.gov/ healthyyouth/obesity/facts.htm

36   Holt DJ, Ippolito P.M., Desroches DM, Kelley CR. *Children's Exposure to TV Advertising in 1977 and 2004. Information for the Obesity Debate.* Federal Trade Commission, Bureau of Economics Staff Report, June 1, 2007. Retrieved October 30, 2014 from http://www.ftc.gov/sites/default/files/documents/reports/childrens-exposure-television-advertising-1977-and-2004-information-obesity-debate-bureau-economics/cabebw.pdf

37   Desrochers DM, Holt, DJ. Children's Exposure to Television Advertising: Implications for Childhood Obesity. *Journal of Public Policy & Marketing* 2007; 26(2):182–201.

tising exposures, a media that has proven nearly impossible to regulate on computers, smartphones, and tablets. In fact, kids are nearly saturated by advertising yet so absorbed in the content it accompanies that they seem to have no defense against its effects.

Even parents who are aware of the powerful effects of media and advertising and take significant steps to protect their children from exposure are unable to negate the influences completely. For seven years, my daughter-in-law, Jennifer, was a nanny for a child of two conscientious parents. One of the parents' rules was that their child was not allowed to watch television. Imagine trying to enforce that expectation in your household. The one exception was that he could watch with his nanny her favorite show, Northern Exposure, in daytime syndication. One of the commercials continually running during the program was for the hair growth product Rogaine. The commercial started with a 30-something man struggling in a soccer match. Clearly his confidence is down because of a receding hairline and a bald spot on the top of his head.[38] After applying Rogaine, his hair is noticeably thicker, and he goes on to score the winning goal.

A few days later, Jennifer and the young boy were kicking the ball around in the backyard, when he shot hard past Jennifer and into the net. He then proceeded to slide on the ground in the fashion of all the great goal scorers and shout at the top of his lungs, "Rogaine!" Score one for the advertisers and marketing team.

Children are not the only vulnerable population on which the media concentrates. Halfway through the great recession of 2008, a University of Michigan study through the National Poverty Center concluded that 14.3% of all Americans lived in poverty. A staggering 25.8% of African Americans, nearly 3 times more than their Caucasian counterparts (9.4%), were at or below the poverty line. As the economy slowly recovers from this devastating recession, many blacks find themselves further behind as their unemployment rates continue to grow disproportionately in contrast to whites.

According to Princeton University professors Michele Lamont and Virag Molnar, the authors of "How Blacks Use Consumption to Shape Their

---

38   Premature balding doesn't seem to be a performance problem for Wayne Rooney who, despite being follicly challenged, has scored 200 goals in one of the most prominent professional soccer leagues in the world. Such is his dominance, he has been named "best footballer" by numerous publications and sport governing bodies.

Collective Identity: Evidence from marketing specialists,"[39] the black consumer represents a unique market for those seeking to advance commercialism. Their interviews with the marketing specialists who target black audiences revealed that the consumption habits of African Americans, spurred on by social comparison to other races, are often an attempt to counteract a real gap in income and resources. According to marketing specialists, the "buying habits of blacks ... [are] strongly guided by a desire to be recognized as equal and fully participating members of society and to disprove the stereotype of blacks as belonging to an underclass deprived of buying power." Remember that this racial class, despite considerable and remarkable advancements, is operating in a society that once quantified them as 3/5 of a person, restricted their basic rights including their ability to own property and vote, and created separate and inferior places for them to attend school, participate in recreation, and buy goods and services. It is not surprising that in a culture trumpeting equal opportunity some blacks may feel like they have something to prove.

Although the desire for social membership and broadcasting one's buying power through the acquisition of expensive things is common among consumers, marketing specialists say blacks' consumer behavior with relation to their income highlights a lucrative level of commitment on the part of the black consumer. Lamont and Molnar note that "despite their lower median household income and lower household expenditures in a lot of product categories, black households outperform white households in pouring money into status consumption."

Indeed, some disadvantaged blacks, like members of every other disadvantaged group, hope to level the playing field with commodities in order to compete with those whose life evaluations are higher due to their advanced income. Even the predominately black musical genres of rap and hip-hop, forged in the fires of the ghettos of America's largest cities, have evolved from explicitly and effectively expressing the outrage of the underclass to adopting and deifying the possessions of those who were once considered oppressors. We have come full circle when artists such as the Australian-born Lorde creates a chart-busting sensation by satirizing the very music once considered the epitome of anti-establishment. In her song, "Royals," written and first performed at the tender age of 15, she rejects the current state of hip-hop, "But everybody's like Cristal, Maybach,

---

39   Lamont M, Molnár V. How Blacks Use Consumption to Shape their Collective Identity. Evidence from marketing specialists. *Journal of Consumer Culture* 2001; 1(1):31–45.

diamonds on your timepiece; jet planes, islands, tigers on a gold leash. We don't care; we aren't caught up in your love affair."

This love affair, this desire to consume more than one's means can support is not reserved solely for the disadvantaged. Nor do forms of media advertise merely to the downtrodden. The largest audience for media seeking to play off of social comparison and the consequent inferior life evaluations generated is the middle class. One of the ramifications of the middle class attempting to obtain possessions deemed necessary by the media is the fact that living paycheck to paycheck is no longer a reality only for minimum-wage earners. A March 15, 2010 analysis by Gary Langer of an ABC World News poll notes that among the 45 percent of Americans who classify themselves as middle class, four in 10 said they were struggling to hang on to that status.

Thus, borrowed money, in the form of credit cards and loans, is how the luxuries that traditionally accompany great wealth are purchased by ordinary folks. Large, lavish homes, multiple brand-new vehicles, and frequent spending sprees are commonplace among the middle class, who strive incessantly to pay off these superficial tokens of opulence rather than do without and risk a drop in their commercialized status.

Perhaps nowhere has such aptly targeted marketing and reckless commercialism occurred than with the United States mortgage lending crisis of the late 2000s. According to Paul Kalra, author of *The American Class System: Divide and Rule*, "Home ownership provides the connecting link between the middle and the upper class."[40] Scores of people leap into lifelong debt to achieve home ownership and its associated status, offering banks and brokers the reward of steady monthly income for the life of a mortgage. The CEOs of these major lending organizations, including those represented by the government, made out like bandits. The team responsible for managing Fannie Mae earned $200 million in income from 1998 to 2003. Like a snake eating its tail, more and more representatives of the industry were willing to engage in unethical behavior in order to reap the temporary benefits. The Mortgage Asset Research Institute claims that "from 2000 to 2006, the number of reported cases of mortgage fraud grew from 3,500 to 28,000.[41]"

---

40   Kalra P. *The American Class System: Divide and Rule*. Brooklyn: Antenna Books, 1996.

41   General Accounting Office. *Information on Recent Default and Foreclosure Trends for Home Mortgages and Associated Economic and Market Developments*. GAO-08-78R, October 16, 2007. Retrieved October 30, 2014 from http://www.gao.gov/assets/100/95215.pdf

Subprime loans targeted borrowers with low incomes and low credit scores, offering mortgages made affordable by a tremendously low initial interest rate and advertising home ownership as a no-brainer investment. These individuals were given information, often in colorful and convincing graphs and charts, that their home was a tremendous investment. Even if they struggled to make monthly payments, they would begin to see the dividends pay off immediately. During this housing boom, home prices were appreciating by 5% to 10% per year, easily outpacing average income increases. Buying a home had become the modern version of the gold rush. Some lenders went so far as to borrow the anticipated increase in home value as part of the initial mortgage as a means of allowing cash-strapped families to make their payments. For instance, a home might be appraised at $500,000. The lender would loan the family $600,000, providing them an extra $100,000 to pay off their monthly debt. Since homes were often increasing by 10% a year, this strategy seemed to be a safe bet. After all, the house would be worth more than the original loan of $600,000 in just two years.

These brokers and banks were lending money via prime and subprime loans to consumers with fewer and fewer assets and lower and lower incomes as a means of acquiring more loans to repackage for resale. Many banks didn't care about the inability of homebuyers to repay the loans for they planned to quickly sell them to other investors, who wouldn't know about the true risk that the borrowers presented. With these securities bearing an inflated and bogus triple-A rating, even savvy investors bought into the hype for high, risk-free returns. Initial lenders made millions from hopeful homebuyers who had been convinced of their chance to buy into the American dream despite the obvious disadvantage to them for doing so. When the housing market crashed and adjustable interest rates went soaring, those same hopeful homebuyers found themselves with rising monthly payments and upside-down loans, unable to pay to keep their homes or sell them to settle their debt.

Consider the home buying experience of a close relative of mine. He is the type of person who enjoys making budgets, analyzing spending trends, and building spreadsheets. Armed with income statements, monthly expenses, accumulated debt, and accounting for various expected changes in lifestyle (read: children), it was calculated that he and his wife could afford a home in the $175,000–$195,000 range. Like many smart potential homebuyers, they also decided to get pre-approved for a mortgage in order to become a more attractive buyer to would-be sellers. When they sat down with their mortgage broker to determine how much of a loan the company was willing to shell out, they were dumbfounded. The broker stated that they qualified for a loan upwards of $405,000. My relative quickly responded, "That's great, but how will we find the money to eat." To which the broker countered, "Your ability to eat is not a factor in the mortgage approval process."

It is not hyperbole to say that lives and families were ruined in the Great Recession. According to a 2012 report by the Federal Reserve, the housing market in the United States declined by seven trillion dollars in a six year period. The loss alone is more than the Gross Domestic Product of every country but the United States itself, leading to many anxious nights among the middle class. In contrast, there is one ordinary man whom I am certain hasn't lost a minute of sleep because of his mortgage or home devaluation. That would be my former co-worker and friend, Bob Anderson. His decision to save and buy his home with cash makes him immune to volatile markets, predatory lenders, poor regulation, and consumers extended beyond their means. His home will be there for his family to enjoy regardless of the circumstances. That makes Bob more powerful than those on rungs well above him on the income ladder.

While purchasing a home without taking out a loan may be unrealistic for most, I hope the mortgage crisis has taught many across the world the destructive nature of chasing after items we cannot afford in the pursuit of heightened life evaluation. Indeed, the rate of family savings and paying down debt has increased substantially over the past few years. At the same time, however, advertisers prepare the next wave of targeted marketing campaigns. Despite possible lessons learned, marketers and advertisers continue to up the ante. By 2018, Internet advertising will be poised to overtake TV as the largest advertising segment, according to PricewaterhouseCooper.[42] That means we'll find more ads in places we're not looking for them, in ways that seem less like a commercial and more like "what we're watching, reading, or browsing."

One of the most effective examples of placing a product within the context of a television show or movie occurred during the mega blockbuster E.T., The Extra Terrestrial. In a famous scene, a young boy places a path of Reese's Pieces on the floor in hopes of enticing E.T. to come out of his hiding place. At the time, Reese's Pieces was a relatively unknown sweet especially in comparison to its other candy brethren M&Ms®. Ironically,

42   PriceWaterhouseCooper. Global entertainment and media outlook 2014–2018. Retrieved October 30, 2014 from http://www.pwc.com/gx/en/global-entertainment-media-outlook/data-insights.jhtml

the parent company of M&Ms had first crack at having its product be the centerpiece of the scene but declined. Obviously, this decision would later be one they would come to regret. An article featured in Time Magazine a month after the United States release of E.T. notes that Reese's Pieces sales had jumped 65%.

Advertisers have taken note, and now a viewer is hard pressed to watch any movie or television show without some sort of product integrated into the screen. Numerous studies have shown that advertising is often most effective when individuals are unaware that they are being solicited. Instead, they surround the product with images that generate positive feelings. James Bond drives around in his BMW Z3 or Aston Martin DB5 playing out every heterosexual male's fantasy of thwarting the bad guy, having sex with the most beautiful girls, and doing so without ever wrinkling his designer tuxedo.

Then there is Acura. Possibly in response to feeling left out of the James Bond party, the Japanese car maker has teamed up with Marvel to advertise their line of sporty and luxury automobiles. The most notable: Robert Downey Jr., aka Tony Stark, aka Iron Man, riding off into the sunset after vanquishing the enemy and saving the world in his sleek Acura NSX. The movie in question, The Avengers, rustled up over $1.5 billion in ticket sales worldwide, according to Boxofficemojo.com.

Companies spend billions of dollars not only on advertising but on organizations whose sole purpose is to better hawk the goods of their client. Consider this explanation about such media planners from the website admedia.org: "Media planning helps you determine which media to use—be it television programs, newspapers, bus-stop posters, in-store displays, banner ads on the web, or a flyer on Facebook. It also tells you when and where to use media in order to reach your desired audience." To understand this concept more fully, let's take a moment to examine how the giants in the information age—Google, Apple, and Facebook—are changing the landscape of advertising by using the information you willingly (maybe unwittingly) supply. Every time you click on Google and use its engine to search the Internet,[43] the sites you enter are recorded by the company. While it might be nice to have customized results based on your preferences ("Hey, how did Google know I am a big sushi fan from Tulsa?"), it comes at a cost to your privacy. An accumulation of all the websites a person has visited provides a detailed profile about the individual and insights that person may not wish to be a part of the public domain. Apple contributes

43   Who can resist the cute, clever, and timely ways Google designs its name for its
        Internet search engine?

to this omnipresent sensation by inserting applications in itssmartphones that can potentially track our partialities, spending habits, net worth, network of friends and family, and even our location. This information, first highlighted by the confidential document leaked by CIA civilian contractor Edward Snowden and later confirmed by the Obama Administration, has been sequestered by the National Security Agency for the all-encompassing purposes of national security. If you plan on committing a crime in the near future, you should probably turn off your phone first or any other device that generates a personal profile. Better yet, make like Stringer Bell in The Wire and stash it in a dumpster because the GPS tracking system in your tablet and phone is uncannily accurate.

Most cavalier of all may be Facebook, which actually boasts about the advertising profiles it creates from users' information. The opening line of Facebook's Advertising Policy states, "At Facebook, we believe that ads should contribute to and be consistent with the overall user experience. The best ads are those that are tailored to individuals based on how they and their friends interact and affiliate with the brands, artists, and businesses they care about." So, by collecting all these statistics about you and your closest 300 friends, Facebook is actually doing you a favor. It would be one thing if this data mining was done solely for the consumer's advantage because the results do provide convenient and practical benefits when sorting through millions of websites to find one specific item. We must also be aware, however, that our Internet histories are being sold for the purposes of more effectively scratching our itchy shopping trigger finger. How else do you think these corporations can offer their services essentially for free to the 99% and still be some of the most profitable in the world?

If these companies are spending more than the GDP of most countries in Africa just to develop these technologies, then the question remains: How much of your personal resources are you committing and whom are you employing to help you counteract the negative influences of media? The answers are likely "zero" and "no one."

As if your lack of protection weren't scary enough, keep something in mind the next time you walk into your favorite store. Increasingly, large retail chains are implanting Radio Frequency Identification chips (RFIDs) into merchandise sold in their stores. These devices are practically invisible, yet have serious implications. RFID chips provide instantaneous information about the amount of a product in the store, where the product is located, and how much of the product is sold. This up-to-the-minute status is revolutionizing how businesses conduct marketing, sales, and inventory.

As a side benefit, these RFID chips also reduce instances of shoplifting and employee theft. At the cost of only five cents per chip, RFID chips can be placed in anything and everything. That fact has Katherine Albrecht and others like her concerned. Ms. Albrecht is the director of the organization Consumers against Supermarket Privacy Invasion and Numbering. She claims that since products in stores and many states' drivers' licenses use the same RFID technology, stores could use both sets of information transmitted by the RFID chips to determine a list of the items you prefer to buy. Armed with your preferences, stores can predict your buying habits and stock the shelves accordingly.

Phillip K. Dick was the futurist whose short stories and novels warned of a society consumed with technological advancements such as RFID chips without the consideration of their myriad misuses. Avid readers of science fiction would undoubtedly place Philip K. Dick in the pantheon of great writers of the genre. His works have inspired many films that you have likely seen: Blade Runner, Total Recall, Paycheck, Screamers, Scanner Darkly, Next, Minority Report, and The Adjustment Bureau. In the critically acclaimed and financially successful film adaptation of Minority Report, directed by Stephen Spielberg and starring Tom Cruise, the protagonist of the film exists in a near future where violent crime can be predicted. As part of this future, there are advertisements that literally seek you out with tailor-made messages, thanks to sophisticated retinal recognition software. In one scene, Cruise walks through a mall covered by walls of three-dimensional advertising. On the walls are sensors that scan the eyes of the passing pedestrians. One of the screens calls out, "John Anderton [Tom Cruise's character], you could use a Guinness right about now." He probably could, as police officers are chasing him (using the same technology that makes these advertisements possible) with the goal of imprisoning him for life. Another ad, this time from American Express, indicates that he has been a member since 2037. When Anderton walks into the Gap, the cybernetic woman greeting him knows exactly what he purchased the last time he was in the store.

While we are no closer to being able to predict when or how crimes like murder will occur, the advancements in advertising highlighted by RFID chips suggest that the described interaction from Minority Report will soon no longer be in the realm of science fiction. This reality will mean that each one of us will have to develop stronger and more adaptive armor to protect ourselves from the influence and power of advertising. How we evaluate the quality of our life may well be at stake.

Though a person making a yearly income of $75,000 is likely to experience the same amount of daily joy and happiness as the not-so-average member of the 1%, he or she is likely to view life as less satisfactory. By the content of television shows, movies, and websites, unceasing media coverage of celebrities, and a torrent of advertisements, we are conditioned to believe that power and success equal having an abundance of expensive things, exclusive access, and an absence of flaws, weaknesses, or unmet desires. Possession of a big house, luxury car, or brand-name wardrobe is symbolic of a life well-lived. Celebrities are idolized and imitated. Consuming products, from makeup and processed foods to wireless phones and a college education, is advertised as the surefire route to obtaining power and achieving fulfillment. Moreover, many women would spend their weight in gold on makeup, gym memberships, cosmetic surgeries, and clothing to make their beauty match that which the average supermodel possesses at birth. They pursue these futile means almost incessantly, ever intrigued and convinced that the next advertised solution they try will work.

These offerings are all too often wolves in sheep's clothing, promising the trappings of "the good life" to people who are perfectly happy in their daily undertakings but are desperate to overcome perceived inferiorities and inadequacies. Predatory lenders let a poor person buy a home until, in accordance with the fine print, terms change and the borrower's monthly payment jumps so drastically that (s)he risks losing the home. Credit seems harmless until a debtor falls behind in payments and repossession relieves him or her of a car, bed, or flat-screen television. Keeping up with the Joneses seems worthwhile until a job loss or illness eliminates a means of earning income and we lose the competition upon which we'd placed our self-worth. Faced with the next advertised mirage of power, those who are in the 99% buy and buy again. After all, the mirage continues to be offered, with our life evaluation weighing in the balance.

Power Points

- While an *income threshold* exists suggesting that a person making $75,000 is likely to experience as much day-to-day happiness as an individual making millions of dollars, it does *not* apply to *life evaluation*, the perception of how our life is progressing, and how much we have achieved.

- Although overflowing with useful and pro-social applications, companies use *media formats* to create a climate of decreased personal satisfaction with the *consumer* and then generate a profit by associating their products with positive life evaluations.

- This strategy of associating products with positive life evaluations is especially employed on the most vulnerable in society—children and underrepresented minority groups—who are most susceptible to the need of *portable status symbols* to prove their worth.

- Faced with the overwhelming onslaught of "buy more" messaging, consumers often overextend themselves monetarily (most notably in the case of the recent *mortgage crisis*) creating a scenario in which they are living paycheck to paycheck or are one life event away from financial ruin.

- Using a slew of advanced tools such as *market planning, Internet profiles, GPS tracking,* and *RFID chips,* companies better personalize their advertising and, in the process, blur the lines of privacy.

- While companies allocate billions of dollars in advertising in an attempt to relieve the consumer of his or her cash, the members of *the 99%* expend minimal amounts of time or resources protecting their assets from this sophisticated marketing machine.

Next Destination

In Chapter 7, we will explore how members of the 99% can begin to build the necessary armor to protect themselves from the effects of social comparison perpetuated by media programming and advertising. The inspiration for the material of this armor likely will surprise you.

7

Lessons from Children

Rule of the Road: Forge your armor out of resiliency.

Mile Markers: War Zone, Trauma, PTSD, Suicide, Dutch Levees, Bounce Back, Magical Thinking, Easy Temperament, Vulnerability, Consumer Nation, George Foreman, Mentoring, Open Communities, Persistence, Tree of Resiliency, Self-Evaluation, Exploitive Culture

In the days and months after that game-changing ride home from Bob, I began to ponder how I might go about amending my own life to better reflect the principles first emphasized in my youth and latter reinvigorated by the example of this modest soul. As someone who had firsthand experience with poverty and minimal assets, I was surprised at how quickly I had bought into the desire to demonstrate to outsiders that here was a man who exceeded his humble beginnings. Now that I was equipped with a new self-awareness, would this knowledge translate into real and lasting change? Temptation to buy and consume in an attempt to feed the appetite of my self-worth would always be in abundance. A thought slowly emerged and then became a drumbeat in my mind, "I'm going to need to develop some armor to protect myself from the army of merchants who hawk their products ensuring happiness and satisfaction." What would be strong enough to withstand the multitudes of advertisements, sales pitches, peer pressures, and never-ending promises?

It would need to come from a material readily available in the landscape of humankind. It would be several years later and on one of my travels thousands of miles away that I would begin to put the pieces together. Finding this suitable substance, however, would prove to be more perilous than I expected.

There is at least one moment in every person's life that (s)he wonders how (s)he got themselves into this predicament. One of my moments came when I found myself huddled inside the hull of a Russian military cargo plane wearing a flak jacket and clutching an army-grade helmet. Well into my 50s and flying into a war zone, the image of Jonah sitting in stunned silence inside the belly of a whale occupied my mind. When we landed at the United Nations-controlled airport, the reasons for the military plane, flak jacket, and helmet became clear: The runway was a pockmarked canvas of asphalt besieged by the daily shelling of a relentless adversary. The airport itself bore the markings of the blind destructiveness of war, most notably the piles of sandbags feebly filling the holes of blown-out walls. While the eyes were assaulted with pictures too chaotic to fully comprehend, it was the cacophony of noise that was most insulting to the senses. The sheer volume of the explosions, accompanied by the sound of mortar shells as they whistled through the air, nearly rendered me incapacitated. I was relieved to jump into an "Egyptian taxi" (provided by the Egyptian military contingency) just to escape the noise even though it was, statistically speaking, the most dangerous part of my passage.

The city streets, once bustling with the life of a thriving metropolis, were abandoned and silent. My driver apologized for the hurried and bumpy nature of his driving but expressed the importance of reaching our destination before nightfall. Once the sun set, the city would fall into complete darkness. Electricity was a rare luxury, and even if that were not the case, any artificial light simply illuminated targets for snipers. With the remaining glimmer of the day seeping through the tiny bulletproof window, I was able to witness the skeletal rows of houses, overturned cars and buses, and a stray dog with its ribs showing through the skin, sniffing purposefully through the rubble in search of food. Our own journey took us through what was known as Sniper Alley to the only operational hotel in town. This formerly lavish Holiday Inn served as a makeshift headquarters for journalistic activities as many major news networks had their reporters anchored there. The inside of the hotel greeted us with pitch blackness, and only through one hallway could I make out a dim glow shining through paper-covered glass. This room served as the guest registration office. Using a penlight, we slowly made our way through the hallway to where the clerk was waiting. Noting our reservation, she presented herself with the decorum of a concierge at the Ritz Carlton. Instead of highlighting the local attractions and the various dining options, however, she informed us that there currently was no electricity or running water in the hotel. She directed me to the stairway and warned that on the fifth level—where my room was located—there was a large hole in the flooring courtesy of a grenade explosion. She mentioned that the location of the rooms was worth the inconvenience of potentially falling through this hole since they offered a restricted city view. In a building often the recipient of artillery fire, a room without a view was a plus. As we parted ways for the night, she promised to send up four bottles of water for washing purposes in the morning. She implored me not to drink it.

Like most Americans, I knew little of the Republic of Bosnia-Herzegovina before it declared independence from Yugoslavia in March of 1992. When the violence erupted shortly thereafter, I was one of millions across the world who watched in silent horror at the daily atrocities funneling through the television screen. Through a series of events combining chance and perhaps divine intervention described in more detail in a previous book[44], I found my life intertwined with those most devastated by this ethnically-charged civil war. Over the next three and a half years, I would travel to Bosnia 15 times. My principal mission, and that of my mental health team, was to work with the group most exploited and vulnerable when powerful adults fail to settle their differences peacefully: children.

From my own early life experiences in Delhi and my work with traumatized children in the United States, I had a keen awareness of the problems I could expect to encounter among the Bosnian youth. No one, however, can ever be completely prepared for witnessing tragedy experienced by children. I encountered issues that I had only read about but never seen. Several of the young people's growth had been physically stunted by the atrocities they had observed. One seven-year-old girl's hair turned gray after her father was killed. Other symptoms included children who learned to fear the light instead of the dark. As I had learned at the hotel, light meant snipers could take aim and fire. Another boy would often rush into the basement of his house the middle of the night, confusing the snoring of his grandfather with the mortar fire engulfing the neighborhood. Of

44   Husain SA. *Hope for the Children: Lessons from Bosnia*. Tuzia, Bosnia-Herzegovina: Behram-Begova Medresa. 2001..

the 791 Bosnian children our research team evaluated, 25% had been shot at by snipers and 71% had a family member who'd been killed. Seventy-seven percent reported trouble sleeping while a similar percentage replied in the affirmative to the statement, "I hate myself." Most disturbingly, an astonishing 92% reported having thoughts of killing themselves compared to nine percent of their peers who had not been exposed to such extreme stress.

This phenomenon is not just reserved for children or the people of Bosnia. In fact, the response to trauma is remarkably universal. The psychological impact of the 2004 tsunami that swept through Indonesia and other parts of Southeast Asia, claiming the lives of 230,000 people, was nearly as devastating for the survivors. Those spared the towering walls of water were left with ruined homes, dead loved ones, and shattered dreams. Upwards of 39% of those exposed to the event suffered symptoms associated with post-traumatic stress disorder (PTSD) including difficulty sleeping, recurring nightmares, increased anxiety and depression, and thoughts of suicide. In the United States, reports of PTSD were also prevalent among those forced to carry on after such devastating disasters as the Oklahoma City bombings, the World Trade Center terrorist attack, and Hurricane Katrina.

Even the most highly trained and battle-tested cannot escape the horror that accompanies trauma. According to military statistics, as of September 5, 2014, 128,496 incident cases of PTSD have been reported in service members deployed since 2000.[45] The actual number enduring this psychological disease is likely much larger, considering the stigma of weakness still attached to this malady. Because of the prevalence of PTSD and depression, the armed forces have seen a dramatic spike in suicides since the onset of the Iraq and Afghanistan wars. A report was released by the military in June of 2012 indicating that 154 servicemen and women had committed suicide in the previous five-month period versus 130 killed in combat during this same time. This finding means more U.S. troops died by their own hand than were killed by the enemy. It is becoming apparent that eroding mental health is a greater danger to our combat forces than any weapon deployed by our adversaries.

---

45   Fischer H. *A Guide to U.S. Military Casualty Statistics: Operation New Dawn, Ope-Fischer HA. A Guide to U.S. Military Casualty Statistics: Operation Inherent Resolve, Operation New Dawn, Operation Iraqi Freedom, and Operation Enduring Freedom. Congressional Research Service, November 20, 2014. Retrieved April 18, 2015 from https://www.fas.org/sgp/crs/natsec/RS22452.pdf*

These sad stories and overwhelming statistics, however, are not without hope. Within the core of many of these survivors is the quality of resiliency that allows them to recover and live normal, content lives. Resiliency's root comes from the Latin resilíre, defined as "to leap back." A person exhibiting resiliency possesses the ability to face and eventually overcome trauma and hardship.

While explaining the concept of resiliency in the various training workshops I have conducted worldwide, I often invoke the spirit of the Netherlands. The Dutch and their predecessors have been fighting a multi-millennium-old battle to curb the harmful effects of the bordering North Sea. Over this period of time, a series of increasingly sophisticated dikes have been built to keep the stormy seas at bay. Land that would otherwise be uninhabitable due to the whims of the North Sea now houses over 50% of the Netherlands' population. In their web article, "Dikes of the Netherlands,"[46] Marshall Brain and Robert Lamb have a passage that serves as a wonderful metaphor when discussing trauma and resiliency: "Much of the Dutch levee system relies on the understanding that levees require regular maintenance, constant monitoring, and a long-term appreciation for how rivers, oceans, and storms behave. When these are in place, communities can thrive safely alongside the beauty and convenience of coastal and riverside areas. It's when we fail to remember this that rivers and oceans become destroyers."

Appropriating this explanation as a metaphor for resiliency, the omnipresent North Sea represents the relentless forces of stress. The Dutch dikes and levees represent a person's ability to manage and push back this stress. With the proper nurturing and support, these tools can be used to fortify one's resiliency. With this resiliency, a healthy and satisfying life can be gained despite the barrage of trauma. If one takes for granted the destructive force of stress and trauma, he or she can be swept up in a tide of depression and despair.

In this vein, I found numerous testimonies to the power of resiliency among the children of Bosnia. Many whose physical development was stunted had attained normal growth once the daily stress subsided. The girl whose hair was permanently gray was thriving in school, and her fear of exploded shells had diminished. Therein lies the most remarkable characteristic of children—their astonishing capacity to bounce back. For many children, it takes very little, perhaps only some words of understanding, to

---

46 Brain M, Lamb R. What is a levee? How Stuff Works, September 4, 2005. Retrieved October 30, 2014 from http://science.howstuffworks.com/engineering/structural/levee2.htm

help them tap into their ability to heal. I saw this resiliency again and again in Bosnia, emerging in the most unexpected circumstances, as flowers will emerge though cracks in a sidewalk.

One advantage that children have in the area of resiliency is the use of tools that would call into question one's sanity if an adult were to employ a similar strategy. One of these tools is magical thinking. Magical thinking is a term that describes children's belief that their wishes and thoughts can control reality. Some of the 7 to 10-year-old boys I came across in the Bosnian capital of Sarajevo provided a textbook example. These children had become experts on artillery. Exposed to the various sounds of the guns used by snipers and soldiers, they could differentiate the make, size, and location of each gun. Most of these weapons were tucked into the surrounding hills of Borije, Poljne, Trebevic, Vraca, Jeverjesko Groblje, and Zuc. Nicknames emerged that originated from the gun's locale. When they heard the retort of a particular cannon, they would say to each other, "Oh, that one's Poli (from Poljine); he can't get us here." As they became experts at this game, it allowed them a feeling of control over their lives and helped reduce the negative psychological impact of living in fear.

Play is also a natural way to express fear and work out problems during childhood. Much of a child's healing process occurs through play. I would observe the Bosnian children in schoolyards acting out scenes from the war around them. Sometimes, they pretended to be soldiers, including brothers and uncles, liberating their city. Regardless of the circumstances, they were always brave, either "winning" or successfully escaping dangerous situations. At one school, we watched two groups of children acting out the sniper attacks from days before. One child play-acted that he had been wounded by a sniper. Two other children took on the role of doctor, swiftly addressing the victim's wounds, and carrying him to safety.

These plays allowed the children of Bosnia to express their anxiety and elicit some control over extraordinary events. Unfortunately, while their stories on the playground always culminated in a happy ending, their real lives were often not as kind. Thankfully, many of the Bosnian children, now young adults, have bright prospects and may even be stronger because of the experience. To say all will do so, however, paints too rosy a picture and glosses over significant details. Not all of the young people I had the privilege to meet were able or will be able to return to some semblance of normalcy.

This fact is a reflection of all our experiences. We know people who seem to trudge through life regardless of the circumstances or obstacles thrown in their path. They may experience moments of feeling down, but these emotions are temporary as their recovery fully takes hold. Then, there are those who seemingly never shake the burdens of life as if their feet are stuck in quicksand. In distinguishing between these two categories of people, the level of developed resiliency serves as the tipping point for failure and success. Cultivated properly, resiliency becomes the armor worn by an individual to withstand the most challenging of life's devices. So, if this "armor," found in abundance as part of the natural core of the children of Bosnia, was strong enough to allow them to endure the longest siege in human history, then couldn't this human quality be harnessed for other purposes? I was beginning to see the importance of mining this core resiliency to enact the necessary change in my life and that of the 99% attempting to reclaim their own personal power. Couldn't this be the source to shield us from the feelings of inferiority, the urge to socially compare, and the compulsion to spend that are omnipresent in a consumer culture?

Like many human characteristics, the seeds of resiliency are planted in early childhood. To be precise, one's predisposition to be resilient starts at conception. The groundbreaking research of child psychiatrist Stella Chess and her colleagues[47] examined the traits children are born with and how they begin to interact with the new world surrounding them. She and her associates then followed these infants as they grew into adolescents and young adults. Based on her study, Chess was able to discern nine characteristic categories known as temperaments exhibited by the infants. The temperaments are

- activity;

- mood;

- intensity;

- distractibility;

- regularity;

- adaptability;

- sensory threshold;

- rhythmicity; and

- approach/withdrawal.

---

47   Thomas A, Chess S, Birch HG. The Origin of Personality. *Scientific American* 1970; 223(2):102–109.

All of the identified traits affect the child's ability to develop resiliency. Take, for instance, the temperament category rhythmicity, the regularity or irregularity of biological function such as sleeping, hunger, and elimination (what time they move their bowels). There are social implications to these simple factors. Parents strongly prefer a child who is regular so that they can schedule their own activity around the predictability of his/her biological demands/needs. A child who is predictable reduces tension between child and caregiver and increases attachment and bonding.

Another category that is relevant to resiliency is approach/withdrawal. A child who readily accepts new situations is referred to as approachable. Those who are approachable are more likely to "roll with the punches" when challenging events present themselves. Children whose initial reaction to new stimulus is avoidance or withdrawal may struggle with the inevitable demands they confront throughout development.

My two sons differed wildly in the approach/withdrawal characteristics, and I have often expressed this dissimilarity with the following hypothetical example: When approaching the edge of a cliff, my oldest son would view it as an exciting new challenge. Without hesitating, he would take a running leap and expect to land in a pristine lake below. My youngest son would stop at the edge of the cliff, take several moments to survey the landscape, and then explore other options to reach the bottom.

The strategies of approach and withdrawal exhibited by my children would face a real world test when both were still under the age of 12. At that time, I received a career opportunity that would require relocating the family to San Diego. My firstborn thought it was a great idea and savored the opportunity for adventure. In contrast, his little brother couldn't have been more horrified at the thought of leaving everything he knew behind. After weighing several factors (most important the desires of those closest to me), we ultimately stayed in Missouri. Many families will face similar scenarios that potentially disrupt routines and lead to dramatic transformations in the immediate environment. The approachable child will be more comfortable with these changes.

Does that mean boys and girls like my youngest son are doomed to live a life pursuing certainty and never foster the resiliency required to face inevitable changes? Not necessarily. A third temperament, adaptability, also plays an important role. After the initial withdrawal response, many children, including my youngest son, are able to adapt to a new situation and eventually become more like an approachable child. In many cases, these individuals are more likely to make good decisions because they carefully approach new situations and control reactionary impulses. The quality of impulsivity can also translate into our decision-making when it comes to purchasing. Big box stores line their checkout aisles with products specifically designated as "impulse buys." Well-schooled merchants focus hours of their work day determining how best to play on our natural impulsivity. Just as it is rational behavior to ensure that there is a lake waiting before one spontaneously jumps from a cliff, it is probably a smart idea to visit multiple dealerships before buying a car.

Another temperament important in the discussion of resiliency is positive or negative mood. Those with a negative mood have a pessimistic outlook on most circumstances. They are the proverbial "glass half empty" individuals. One of my mentors during my early years at the University of Missouri enjoyed telling the parable of "Jane and Tina" to illustrate his point about this temperament spectrum. Jane and Tina were twin girls raised in the same household. Jane never smiled, was constantly worried about world events, and was weighed down by their implications. Tina was the exact opposite, always able to find the silver lining. Concerned that Jane was too gloomy and cynical and that Tina viewed the world with rose-colored glasses, the parents took both to a specialist. As part of the treatment process, the child psychiatrist brought Jane into a room filled with birds chirping, bright colors, and all manner of toys. Conversely, Tina was given a room filled with manure.

A few hours later, the specialist checked in with both children. In the bright-colored room, Jane was sitting in the corner and could not enjoy her surroundings. When confronted about why she felt so down, Jane stated, "With all the starving children in the world, how can I enjoy these beautiful things?" Tina, on the other hand, was running around the room with a smile on her face, showing little concern about the manure. When asked why she remained so happy, Tina stated, "With so much manure around, there must be a pony close by!" The positive-mood child demonstrated high resiliency because she was able to see the bright side of a potential disaster. Applying this scenario to our discussion on media influences, the negatively oriented child will likely struggle to achieve happiness regardless of what she accumulates or consumes. Because she will always be looking externally to fill an internal void with limited success, Jane will be an ideal target for advertisers selling products promoting heightened self-worth.

As an additional part of their research, Chess and associates looked for commonalities that could be found when examining multiple temperaments. Using the statistical tool of factor analysis, they determined that various combinations of the nine temperaments often created three types of children: easy, difficult, and slow-to-warm up. The easy child has dramatic advantages over his difficult brethren. As Stella Chess followed these children into adulthood, easy children tended to become successful adults. In contrast, those who were categorized as difficult exhibited a higher propensity of emotional disturbance, difficulty with interpersonal relationships, behavior problems, and criminal activity. The categories that are associated with an easy temperament correlate highly with children who have a greater degree of resiliency. Temperament studies have also demonstrated that easy children will carry this natural resiliency into adulthood.

Clearly, those who have a higher degree of resiliency with accompanying qualities of positive self-esteem, problem-solving skills, an optimistic outlook, and a vast support network have a greater probability of overcoming setbacks. However, anybody who is exposed to a severe enough dose of adverse experiences will collapse under the pressure of the hardships. This is where environmental factors come into to play. If environmental factors were a coin, then one side could be called resiliency while the other side could be labeled vulnerability. Put in different terms, resilience and vulnerability are like the opposite ends of a continuum, counterbalancing one another in a delicate dance that at any given time may be weighted more heavily on one side or the other.

Poverty promotes vulnerability, setting a variety of factors in motion that work against an individual in his community. The poor have more exposure to disease and less access to proper medical care. The poor often lack proper nutrition which, especially in children, stunts development and growth. Education is also in shorter supply for those born into poverty, illustrated by the fact that in many countries a learning institution is reserved only for the upper class. Even in countries where education is mandatory for all youth, the quality is often uneven.

A child with fewer physical and emotional resources is more likely to become an adult who is more susceptible to the claims that material possessions will bolster one's self-worth. Take, for instance, the example of the individuals living in the impoverished circumstances described in Chapter 6. Purchasing goods beyond their budgetary means serves the purpose of attempting to satisfy a self-esteem need. In contrast, a child who receives love and attention and whose needs are met in a reasonable and predictable manner develops security and a view of the world as supporting, friendly, and trusting. (S)he is less likely to fall prey to the influence of outside forces promising a bevy of pleasures because (s)he feels internally secure.

Of course, discussing resiliency in relation to the vulnerable or those exposed to war is certainly not an original premise. Much scholarly literature is devoted to how we assist youth in escaping the destructive grasps of the ghettos across the world. Linking resiliency to extraordinary circumstances, however, limits the scope and impact that resiliency can have on those individuals who experienced more "normal" upbringings. Whether or not our children live in impoverished circumstances, it is important to promote resiliency to deal with the negative stimulus that accompanies simply participating in life. What is guaranteed is that our children will at one time or another encounter the playground bully, suffer an achievement setback, or be exposed to an advertisement that will exploit the susceptibility of a still-forming personality.

To promote resiliency and reduce vulnerability to any degree, a well-cultivated support system is vital. The support system begins with the primary caregivers but quickly extends to other family members such as siblings, grandparents, aunts, uncles, and cousins. Neighbors and friends of the family unit can also play an important role. As a child reaches school age, teachers become an increasingly important factor in shaping a child's resiliency. Teachers who help a child approach a new skill with excitement and enthusiasm and possess the patience to work through their student's struggles will instill a sense of perseverance. A teacher can also take the form of a mentor who, instead of practicing his or her craft in a formal classroom, instructs the young person in the more reality-based arena of the community. Mentors can run the gamut of professions from religious leader to high school basketball coach. The quality they share is that they have at heart the best interests and welfare of the individual who comes to them for advice. These mentoring relationships often last throughout a lifetime.

In reading the biographies of many famous and successful people, the subject frequently highlighted is how teachers or mentors were able to provide the right guidance at a pivotal moment. Without their example, words of wisdom, or steady hand, the individual could have experienced quite negatively divergent results. Such is the case for boxing legend George Foreman. Anyone under the age of 40 probably knows Foreman as the happy-go-lucky pitchman who sells grills and has several children, all named a derivative of George. They also are likely aware that, in a remarkable career renaissance, he won the heavyweight boxing title at age 45. During his comeback, George was a crowd-pleasing fan favorite whose jovial personality resonated above a violent sport. What these same admirers may not remember is a younger Foreman who was feared for his vicious punching power and overall aura of brutality.

In his autobiography, By George, he discusses a childhood void of structure and filled with mishap. An astonishingly strong human being, even at a young age, Foreman would beat up the local boys and take whatever money they were carrying. His lifestyle of petty theft and alcohol use was a precursor for larger crimes and possible stints in jail. In a last ditch effort to avoid this fate, George became a member of the Job Corps, where he met a man who would change his life. Charles Broadus, known simply as "Doc," was a respected amateur and professional boxer-turned-trainer. He took one look at the hulking George and realized he had found something special. Broadus was able to help Foreman maximize his considerable physical attributes and channel his rage into a productive endeavor. The result was a fighter who won a gold medal in the 1968 Olympic games, became the heavyweight title holder by dominating the equally prolific Joe Frazier, and amassed a 40–0 record (37 by knockout) before falling to the "rope-a-dope" strategy employed by Muhammad Ali in a match epically titled, "The Rumble in the Jungle."

What is remarkable about Foreman is that his second act has been just as eventful and noteworthy as his first. While many prominent athletes struggle to adjust after their professional careers come to an end, George Foreman remains busy as a boxing commentator, thriving businessman, minister to his church, and philanthropist. The lessons taught to him by Charles Broadus translated outside the ring and throughout multiple stages of Foreman's life. Like most resilient people, Foreman was able to adapt his own personal circumstances to the changing world around him.

Interestingly enough, Broadus shared many commonalities with Foreman. As a youngster growing up in California, Broadus also had a penchant for street fighting. He found his own mentor in Jack Blackburn, the former trainer of Joe Louis. This mentee-turned-mentor transformation is fairly common as the skill of resiliency is passed on from one generation to the next.

Mentoring is a personal, one-on-one relationship, yet social support can take on a more communal form. Often, the pulling together of an entire group or community can be more powerful than the individual attributes of the people involved. In some societies, the entire community takes on the responsibility of rearing children. The "it takes a village to raise a child" approach can have a major impact on building resiliency. Small communities across the world, whose streets are filled with families who have longstanding roots, engage in a multitude of informal gatherings and have a vested interest in the well-being of all households. My wife and I were fortunate to raise our boys in such a neighborhood, and it was comforting to hear the shrieks of glee and laughter of the neighborhood kids running around. The field of play blended from one yard to another. The fear shared by many is that this open philosophy is being replaced by the promise and price tag of safety in the form of gates and fences. While this closed environment may provide a semblance of physical security, it is more than offset by the reduction in emotional security that a tight-knit community can bestow.

Thankfully, nature has left in most children a tool for building prosperity regardless of the surroundings in which they were raised. Stella Chess' research indicated that a plurality of infants are born with an easy temperament. Since an easy temperament—and the warm responses it receives from caregivers—is a robust predictor of resiliency, it means the predisposition to bounce back from adversity is prevalent in many people. This advantage is quite different from most biological endowments that tend to be found in only the top 1%. It is unlikely that you will be as intelligent as Bill Gates or as charismatic and savvy as Oprah Winfrey, but chances are you or your child's natural ability to be resilient is equal to the elite. This ease of accessibility is another major reason why resiliency is the ideal armor to combat the considerable pitfalls of a consumer culture. We can cultivate it in any child, whereas the ceiling for understanding the Chebotarev Density Theorem or writing advanced computer programming is likely predetermined.

What about those who were neither blessed with a temperament that promotes resiliency nor raised by parents or guardians who were able to build this quality in the absence of biological endowment? For these adults to build resiliency, it is important to engage in a process of self-evaluation and reflection. Edith H. Grotberg, Ph.D., Director of the International Resilience Project at the Ciovitan International Center, UAB, has developed a model and assessment instrument for resiliency[48] that I have incorporated in my training and work with disaster victims. The model depicts a tree with three branches representing mental health, social connectedness, and mastery of skills. The self-assessment takes the variables of these areas and rates an individual based on statements that begin with "I am ..." (mental health), "I can ..." (social connectedness), and "I have ..." (mastery of skills). This assessment is actually designed for measuring childhood resiliency;

48   Grotberg E. I AM, I HAVE, I CAN: What families worldwide taught us about resilience. *Reaching Today's Youth: The Community Circle of Caring* 1998; 1(3):36–39.

however, it can be relevant to adults as well. If these conditions or characteristics were not present in childhood, then they reflect gaps in an adult's resiliency potential. The adult is now playing catch-up and should begin to address this underdeveloped area.

The encouraging and hopeful aspect of the "I am," "I have," and "I can" statements is that a person does not have to be an intellectual mastermind or rich tycoon or have a superior build to embody these qualities. For anyone and everyone, these tools are within grasp. Like any skill, they require concentrated practice and development. With this hard work comes tremendous rewards.

To highlight my point, let's examine each branch of the tree in more detail. One "I have" statement is, "I have people who show me how to do things right by the way they do things." Unlike a child, an adult has control over the people with whom they chose to surround themselves. A strong indicator of the health of our current path is how much time we allocate to those who live their life in a manner that is respectful and conscientious as opposed to those who strive for only self-gratification at the expense of others. As mentioned earlier, resilient people have mentors they can trust whose values they can emulate. These mentors provide support and give sincere advice and guidance without seeking promotion or reward.

One "I am" statement is, "I am respectful of myself and others." Resiliency translates into personal attributes and strengths that allow the person to be decent, helpful, and respectful to others. These individuals often hold the title of "border dweller." Throughout history, a border is a conscious designation that separates groups of people. Despite their close proximity, these factions may have quite divergent cultural mores and harbor intense hostilities and rivalries. A border dweller is someone who is competent and accepted in multiple camps among various groups of people. Because they are open-minded and sympathetic, others reciprocate this decency, help, and respect. Thus, when an individual faces a situation of need, he can tap into a vast network of resources and not resort to consulting those whose primary motivation is to use and abuse for personal gain.

This brings us to an "I can" statement: "I can find someone to help me when I need it." Resilient people have no problem asking for help. They build upon pre-existing support systems. The resilient have the self-awareness to understand their strengths and weaknesses. They are willing to ask the difficult questions and don't shy away from confronting parts of their personality that need work. This area is one in which children have a significant advantage over adults. Children are infinitely more malleable than adults and are not only open to guidance, they crave it. Adults, on the other hand, frequently operate under the false premise that maturity equates to being able to accomplish every task or answer every question. In some instances, it benefits us all to be more childlike. To be more specific, it benefits us to be more like the child who has experience with trauma.

In a book about the origins of power, why it is inequitably distributed, and how the 99% can begin to reverse this trend, why spend an entire chapter on the topic of resiliency? By focusing on children, such as those in Bosnia who have experienced the atrocities of war, we can understand the material essential to fortify our own armor. The 99% are unlikely to ever face the intensity of violence and loss encountered by these children. The average person will experience, however, the natural grieving associated with a changing living or occupational environment, the end of a close relationship, and the loss of a loved one. Resiliency will be a major factor in an individual's capacity to overcome these potentially disruptive and painful episodes. The resilient will provide themselves enough time and space to eventually recover without turning to the temporary pain diluters of excessive food, drugs, and material possessions.

Moreover, the need for resiliency transcends the normal events of the life cycle. It is here where the 99%'s connection with the children of Bosnia is more salient. Remarkably, the 99% are attempting to manage their own daily exposure to trauma. Comparing the relative convenience and normalcy of our lives to those of the Bosnian children in the early 1990s is not an attempt to minimize their tragedies or loss. It is foolhardy to believe any of us would trade places with or have our children trade places with the Bosnians during this deadly conflict. Rather, in examining how others have addressed a trauma-infused environment, we can learn how to cope with a society that has a different form of aggressor waiting to storm the gates.

This trauma may not include constant enemy fire, vivid and violent images, or constant fear for one's safety. What it does encompass is a barrage of messaging indicating that, despite our best efforts, we are not intelligent enough, successful enough, good-looking enough, or wealthy enough to be satisfied in this modern world. While this idea may be difficult to accept, the trauma inflicted upon the people of Bosnia has one distinct benefit over the trauma experienced by the 99%: The Bosnians knew they were experiencing something extraordinary. Before war and ethnic cleansing, there existed a period of relative calm and prosperity. The city of Sarajevo was eight years removed from hosting the Winter Olympics. Eventually, and not without numerous fatalities and tremendous suffering, the war concluded and a semblance of stability returned.

Most of the 99% are unaware that they are actually being exposed to trauma. And this brand of trauma has no end in sight. In fact, the manner in which this trauma is proliferated continues to become more sophisticated. What's worse, the 99% are led to believe that the distress and inadequacy they are feeling is of their own creation. One of the mental health priorities of working with children who have been traumatized is to reassure them that the circumstances causing the painful emotions are not their fault. But the 99% are constantly being told that if they buy a particular product, ascribe to certain beliefs, or work harder than their neighbor, the troubles will go away. As a result, we are pitted against one another in an endless competition of who can accumulate and consume more, too often for the profit of the elite and at the expense of our brethren. This competition often has the mystique of building character and strong will. However, in many individuals, it only deepens the void between the real and ideal self. As discussed in Chapter 5, those who cannot reconcile the differences between the real self and the ideal self suffer from a general malaise that eats away at their spirit.

It is the resilient person who possesses the necessary armor to combat the exploitive messaging that is part of every culture. A resilient person is a well-grounded individual. (S)he is a person who will find opportunities regardless of the circumstances and is constantly moving forward. (S)he is comfortable with who (s)he is as a person. The positive self-esteem and general contentment accompanying resiliency bridges the gap between the real self and the ideal self. Advertising has a limited hold on and appeal to these individuals. They have the tools to forge their own path and pursue their own dream free from the propaganda of any celebrity, political party, organization, or corporation. In the children of Bosnia and those who successfully emerged from trauma around the world, I had found a truly human substance strong enough endure the onslaught of a society urging us to constantly consume—a substance that needs no amount of biological endowment, inheritance, or luck to be properly made.

Power Points

- People exposed to prolonged stress or catastrophic events are susceptible to the *trauma*-induced symptoms of intense anxiety, physical deterioration, nightmares, and *suicidal* tendencies.

- *Resiliency* is the ability of individuals to *bounce back* from difficult experiences and hardships. Like any important skill, resiliency must be cultivated in each person regardless of one's perceived *vulnerability* to stress.

- Unlike many biological endowments reserved for the elite, nature favors in the 99% the *temperament* most advantageous for the development of *resiliency.*

- While the seeds of this power supply begin at conception, environmental factors such as *open communities*, access to *mentors* and caring adults, and the willingness to engage in *self-evaluation* are important in the formation of resiliency.

- Although most of the 99% are not inhabitants of a *war zone,* the messaging of inadequacy fueled by a *consumer nation* exposes them to a more covert source of trauma.

- Due to its strength in the face of life's most severe challenges combined with its ease of accessibility, *resiliency* is the ideal material to forge one's armor in the fight against an *exploitative culture.*

Next Destination

A critical step in regaining power requires the 99% to wrestle control of their life stories from those who are attempting to define the narrative for their own personal gain.

Syed Arshad Husain, M.D. & A. Darius Husain

8

Reclaiming the Narrative

Rule of the Road: If you don't like the ending, rewrite the story.

Mile Markers: Charter Schools, At-Risk Youth, Graduation, Transformation, Narrative Therapy, Competing Storylines, Re-Authoring, Counter-files, Social Media, George W. Bush, Barack Obama, Manifest Destiny, Language Extinction, Reflective Questions, Cross-Generational

On the first Wednesday of every month for the past 14 years, an open house has taken place for students interested in a charter school located in the heartland of the United States. For many in the room, while they may not know it at the time, their decision to attend this orientation will reshape the course of their lives. Despite this significant outcome, the open houses have occurred with little advertisement and fanfare. There are no elaborate videos or PowerPoints. The person running them forgoes the customary shirt and tie and often can be found wearing the gym clothes he donned to play basketball with his students earlier in the day. He doesn't even bother to offer refreshments or a tour of the school unless directly asked. Instead, he starts the open house with two simple statements and one lofty promise. He states, "Everyone in this room has something in common: You are here because you have been unsuccessful in school; and I imagine this has been going on for a long time." This bluntness by a complete stranger is often met by its audience with lowering eyes of shame and uncomfortable silence.

Pausing long enough to allow the words to sink in yet not so long as to precipitate a mass exodus, he follows up with a second statement. "You have another thing in common. Despite this lack of success, you haven't given up on your hopes and dreams." Invariably, the eyes begin to rise and the participants sit a little straighter. Then comes the promise: "I don't care what your past history might be, if you make the commitment to give your best effort, I promise you will walk out of this school with a high school diploma and a chance to attend college." Not surprisingly, 95% of the people in attendance fill out the form indicating their interest in enrolling.

The school's mission is to graduate youth most at risk for dropping out of high school. Most of its students previously attended a large high school in the surrounding metropolitan area. Almost all come from poverty and have been exposed to tragedies of life that no child should have to experience. Deaths of immediate family members, physical and emotional abuse, witnessing of extreme violence, and persistent hunger are not uncommon. A few have been known to spend their nights in a car. As a result, truancy, drug use, teen pregnancy, gang affiliation, troubles with the law, anxiety, and depression are prevalent. The school works on a dual track to address their social/emotional needs while building their academic skills. The staff possesses an appropriate educational background and receives ongoing training in both core subject areas and the basic principles of psychology and counseling. Students are approached with the helper's creed of unconditional positive regard. Because the enrollment is limited to 70 students, class sizes remain small and it is nearly impossible to slip through the cracks.

The results have been remarkable. Attendance rates often double and sometimes triple that of their previous schools. Reading and math scores remain competitive without even taking into consideration that many of the students experienced chronic truancy since elementary school. Graduation rates mirror the state averages despite the fact that 95% of the students are at least one semester behind in credit and most are one to two years behind their class. The school has managed to achieve Adequate Yearly Progress (AYP) in every area identified by the infamous No Child Left Behind legislation. This unique place of learning has been lauded for closing the elusive "achievement gap" for free/reduced school lunch students and young men and women of color. Most important, the environment has that positive vibe and culture that any experienced educator can feel by spending just five minutes in the building.

The buy-in to the program starts at the open house, which serves as one bookend of a student's participation in the school. The capstone event, and what truly drives the continued will of the students and staff, is the graduation ceremony. Seventy percent of the students who are enrolled in the school for at least three months will fulfill the state-mandated requirements for earning a high school diploma. While the open house may be characterized by subtlety and understatement, the graduation festivities are a spectacle not to be missed. Two hundred people cram into a banquet hall at a local church to cheer on their daughter, son, grandchild, niece, nephew, cousin, friend, classmate, or acquaintance. Random exclamations of joy spontaneously resonate from the crowd, reminiscent of a Baptist revival. After all, almost everyone in attendance once believed this day would never come in his or her lifetime.

As part of the proceedings, each graduate prepares and delivers a speech summarizing his or her time and growth at the school. Their words cover the intense and personal struggles that each have faced during this quest for a diploma. They highlight the moment where things began to turn around for them, and these include a laundry list of people who assisted them in reaching their potential. The speeches are filled with hope and promise as they describe their plans for the future including acceptance to college, a job correlated to their interests, or a commitment to military service. In essence, their addresses to an audience of those who know them best are meditations on the limitlessness of the human spirit. Though this description may sound like hyperbole, it is impossible not to be deeply moved by their emotion-laden words, and Kleenex boxes are strategically placed throughout the hall.

During one graduation I had the privilege to attend, I heard from a young man who had lived on his own since he was 15. He was effectively orphaned, not by an untimely death but by the choice of the woman who birthed him. He said, "My drive to graduate was always about proving to my mom she was wrong about me. I wasn't a failure. I could make something of my life. I imagined standing here and rubbing this accomplishment in her face. Now that I have made it, I would tell her I still love her even though she couldn't always love me like she should. And I would let her know she is forgiven and hope she would be proud of me."

Another student told the story of how she pleaded to God to let her baby live. The stress of being 16 and pregnant likely led to her little girl being born ten weeks premature. They weren't sure if the child would survive. The young woman asked for divine intervention, and, in return, she promised to live her life differently. She would set the right example for her daughter and pursue her education and career aspirations with earnest. Because her little girl had recently celebrated her second birthday healthy and happy, she viewed her graduation as simply keeping up her end of the bargain.

Once the students concluded, there was time set aside for parents and family members to approach the microphone and bask in the glory of this singular moment. We heard from a mother who chronicled her own challenges with school. Neither she nor the student's father was able to graduate from high school. Her son was transcending the family history and setting the standard that she knew her other sons would eventually follow. Another parent, clearly not accustomed to public expressions of emotion, only spoke for 20 seconds but his words reverberated throughout the room. Unsuccessfully fighting back the tears pooling in his eyes, he stated, "Sweetheart, I haven't said this enough, especially lately. I love you, and I am thankful to be able to call myself your father."

Listening to his brief statement brought back memories of when my life changed forever with the birth of my son. I had never experienced so much joy, and at the same time, so much fear. Joy surrounding his little sounds, the way he smiled at me, and all the dreams he had yet to even conceive. Fear regarding the dangers he would face, watching over him to make sure he's still breathing while he slept, and concern that I would be a good and strong enough father. I began to feel the devastation these parents must have embodied when it seemed their children were on a path of failure. When you stare in your child's eyes for the first time, the last thought in your mind is that this precious gift could encounter such despair. Then, in the instant you are ready to give in to this despair and lose faith, a dramatic turnaround begins. This elation coupled with relief may cause one to dance right there in the aisle.

After the family members concluded pouring out their hearts with gratitude and praise, a year-in-review slide show was projected on a large screen in the front of the banquet hall. The humorous tone was a nice complement to the emotional catharsis that preceded it. We were all in need of a good laugh. Admittedly, I didn't understand all the inside jokes indicative of a close-knit community. However, it was the pictures that stood out for me more than the colorful commentary. The hard facial lines and slumped postures characteristic of the early photos gave way to genuine smiles and a body language exuding confidence. These graduates physically transformed before my eyes.

By the time the slide show finished and the diplomas were distributed, I was completely energized and rejuvenated. I felt optimistic about our youth and subsequently the future of our society. I couldn't help wondering, however, what might have happened if this school hadn't been made available to these students.

Thankfully, there are many schools across the nation and around the world that have made similar inroads with at-risk populations. What makes these schools different from one another is that their methods and approaches often vary dramatically, from requiring uniforms to using only first names; from highly structured, regimented school days to project-based or online education; from military-style drilling to touchy-feely expression that would make any flower child proud. What they share is an entire population of students, staff, family members, boards of directors, and other stakeholders pulling together in the same direction for the benefit of these youth. They also realize that, regardless of their successes, much more work is left to be done. Humility serves as the antidote to complacency.

One unique feature of many of these schools is that they, without consciously being aware of doing so, employ the foundations of narrative therapy. This conclusion does not imply that students are actively involved in traditional once-a-week counseling. Instead, the principles of narrative therapy are practiced in what is known as a milieu setting. This type of setting is personified by goal achievement through group environments and positive peer support applied in real-life situations. The milieu for the schools are the classrooms, hallways, lobby, gym, and off-campus locations inhabited by the students.

Narrative therapy was developed during the 1970s and 1980s by Michael White and David Epston[49] as an alternative to the prevailing psychological approaches of the day. Unlike many of their peers, White and Epston balked at the idea that mental illness inhabited the body and needed to be treated or removed. They also became increasingly concerned about the dividing of the unhealthy from the healthy through the practice of admissions to hospitals and institutions.

School systems inadvertently practice their own version of division. Most urban schools have a disproportionate number of students who are English as a Second Language Learners (ESL), receive free and reduced-

---

49   See, for example: http://www.narrativetherapycentre.com/narrative.html

price school lunches, and qualify for special education services. Further, within these large educational settings, those who are deemed problematic or low achievers are often shipped off to the local alternative programs.

The charter school whose graduation I attended acted as a de facto alternative program. Its students arrived with a potpourri of problem behaviors: fighting, name calling, bullying, being bullied, truancy, lack of respect for their teachers, vandalism, attention deficit disorder, oppositional behavior disorder, and learned helplessness. Conventional wisdom would suggest that these young men and women had ailments that should be removed, like a cancerous tumor, before they could experience success. In many cases, what is remarkable is that these behaviors never materialized at the school. In fact, the staff rarely bothers to read disciplinary or behavior reports sent with the student because they have proved irrelevant once the setting has changed. These write-ups could actually be damaging as they could serve to label a student or lead to biased behavior on the part of teachers and administration. The school's objective is to provide the structure, nurturing, attention, respect, and supervision that fosters healthy development and renders the maladaptive behaviors unnecessary. This claim is not to imply that all students immediately turn their educational fortunes around when they attend this school. Not all do. When the vast majority of students rarely engage in the misbehavior littered across their academic record, however, we may conclude that perhaps it is not the student who is sick.

Moving away from the concept of the body being mentally unhealthy, White and Epston carried the fundamental belief that their clients held the key to their own positive resolution. Their interest rested in the stories individuals told about themselves and their relation to their environment. These so called "narratives" invariably contained an underlying "problem" that had caused difficulties in the individual's life. By focusing on alternative storylines emphasizing character strengths, the client is able to re-author and reclaim the narrative, thus freeing himself from the problematic themes of his past.

In his book *Theories of Psychotherapy Series: Narrative Therapy*[50] author Stephen Madigan suggests that a skilled narrative therapist understands that the stories we tell about ourselves are rooted in the cultural, political, economic, and familial context surrounding us. Take, for instance, the students attending the open house at the charter school. One storyline of a teenager growing up in the "hood" is failure at school, frequent drug

50   Madigan S. *Narrative Therapy. Theories of Psychotherapy Series*. Washington, DC: American Psychological Association, 2010.

use, troubles with the law, and impregnating or becoming pregnant at a young age. At the same time, these teens live in a society promoting the theme that anyone can make it with hard work and dedication. Ask these students what they want to pursue as careers, and their likely answer will be athletes, rappers, doctors, lawyer, and judges. All are professions requiring considerable skill and exposure to opportunity. The problem occurs when narrative influence #1, "hood" life, and narrative influence #2, "I want to become a doctor," directly come into conflict with one another, as the behaviors presented in #1 significantly reduce one's ability to achieve the goals highlighted in #2. This confusion is further compounded when high profile individuals who have made it out of poverty often romanticize a life centered on drugs, gangs, and violence. These competing and equally relevant storylines leave the individuals disoriented and disillusioned with their future prospects.

To address these feelings of dissatisfaction, the school encourages students to recognize the positive attributes woven into these competing narratives. Part of the re-authoring process for students at the school centers around their continued desire for success despite the considerable factors working against them. Once they start telling their stories, these young men and women are often surprised to see the amount of courage, discipline, and skill they have displayed to achieve what they have accomplished thus far.

Stephen Madigan writes, "Re-authoring conversations invites the clients to help flush out some of the more neglected areas and events of their lives often covered over by the problem story being told. These may include achievements under duress; survival skills growing up; and personal qualities left out of their story such as generosity, ethical stances, and kindness." No longer cast in the role of failure, they view themselves as survivors[51]. No longer allowing their problem narrative of weakness to override their alternative narrative of strength, these students are free to embrace the practices that will garner the rewards they desperately seek. They now have permission to embody the role of "good student," not because the persona of "bad student" was removed like a wart and not because these prosocial characteristics were added on like an appendage. No, they can accomplish this transformation because these qualities always existed within them; they needed only to be drawn out and become a part of their lived reality.

---

51 As one friend told me just recently, "I am no longer a survivor, I'm a thriver. I buried the survivor mentality years ago."

This reality includes increased attendance, higher rates of work completion, and improved relationships with teachers and peers. Over the long run, these actions bring the student closer to the goal of earning a diploma. The graduation and the proceedings themselves celebrate this accomplishment but also serve as an important component of the narrative therapy. One of the tools of a narrative therapist is the letter-writing campaign. In this scenario, individuals close to the client are asked to write letters reinforcing the re-authored narrative. These letters prove to be what Madigan refers to as a "counter-file" to the constant documentation that often attempts to summarize our numerous complexities in a shallow box. While the graduation doesn't necessarily include letters, it fulfills the stated purpose by creating artifacts that defy the previous storyline of low GPAs, test scores, and class ranks. These statistics are replaced by speeches from teachers and loved ones devoted to the considerable obstacles overcome, by pictures depicting happiness and resolve, and by a diploma that states in no uncertain terms, "My future has arrived."

These remarkable transformations on the part of the students of this charter school provide hope for the 99% who are attempting to transcend their own existence. To be able to look within ourselves to find the skills and traits to live a more authentic life, as opposed to being defined by what is expected of us because of our life circumstances, is critical in obtaining a sustainable form of power. The techniques of "re-authoring" are relevant to anyone who ever feels that any portion of his or her life is out of control or heading down the wrong path.

By placing the narrative at the center of their therapeutic emphasis, White and Epston are also acknowledging a fundamental component of the human condition—the overwhelming need to share our stories. In our modern society, the tools to tell the stories of our lives have grown exponentially. With 1.39 billion users, Facebook has become the ultimate forum for communicating with family, friends, and acquaintances about how we spend the day. Had a life-altering thought? You can post it. Had an amazing experience at a concert or a football game? You can post it. Celebrating the birth of your first child? You can post it with a picture. Much to the consternation of those linked to your page, if you had an experience with a barista who put regular milk instead of soy milk in your coffee, you have the ability to rage about it in tremendous detail.[52] The timeline function organizes your personal history, both significant and mundane, from beginning to end in an interactive storybook that has you as the main char-

---

52   One of my relatives likes to call this phenomenon "1st world problems."

acter. As part of its tenth anniversary celebration, Facebook even created a movie of highlights of the previous year tailor-made for each user. We enjoy all of this capacity with no cost and little effort. Nielsen, the prominent ratings company, determined that Americans spent 53.5 billion minutes on Facebook in May 2011 — the collective equivalent of 101,720 years.

Clearly, we are obsessed with the distribution of our own narratives and remaining informed about the narratives of the people to whom we relate. What the 99% often fail to see, however, is the significance of the relationship between power and what emerges as the definitive narrative. Those who seek power and ascend to the echelon of the elite appreciate this concept and become experts in controlling the narrative. This practice is readily seen in the realm of politics at the local, state, and federal level. He or she who commands the audience's attention and tells the most compelling story is almost certain of victory. To understand this statement in its full splendor, one would have to look no further than the rise of the two most recent American presidents.

George W. Bush was not the most likely candidate to be president. Yes, his grandfather was a U.S. Senator for 12 years. Yes, his father was a Member of Congress, Director of the CIA, Vice President to Ronald Reagan, and the 41st President of the United States. He was a member of the nation's political royalty. It was deemed by many, however, that George W. Bush did not possess the qualities or disposition that would lead to success in public office. He had a reputation for drinking too much, including being cited for driving under the influence and having his licensed revoked. His first foray into politics was disappointing as he lost a bid to become a U.S. Congressman in a relatively rural and remote district. George famously described himself as the black sheep of the family to no less than Queen Elizabeth of England. If there were ever to be another Bush to achieve political prominence, the likely candidate was his brother Jeb. Not surprisingly, it would be nearly two decades before he was to toss his hat in the ring again.

At almost 40 years of age, Bush took stock of his life. His business career was mixed, his marriage and connection to his daughters were strained, and his drinking was still an issue. Faced with possibly losing everything of value to him, Bush fundamentally remade himself after a conversation with a prominent religious leader and family friend, Billy Graham. Bush turned his life over to God and embraced Jesus Christ as his savior. He was what evangelicals refer to as "born again." He stopped drinking completely, and his relationship with his wife and children improved.

When Bush decided to run for governor of Texas against the well-established, incumbent Ann Richards, his narrative played an important role in obtaining victory. Richards was a well-respected governor, and Bush had never held any political office. Running as a Republican, he naturally faced daunting odds because 39 of the 45 previous governors of Texas were Democrats. Early predictions of the race anointed Richards in a blowout. Bush went from county to county to tell his story: He was man who had committed many sins, was a blemish on his own family, and had found religion as his salvation. The narrative themes of flawed individual whose devotion to God saved him resonated with the people he encountered in cafes and church halls. In him, they could see themselves. In the end, his storyline of down-to-earth candidate, guided by Christian beliefs, who would protect the rights most sacred to Texans (in this particular election, most notably the ability to carry concealed weapons) won the day. It did not help that Richards' own narrative in the increasingly conservative state morphed into an out-of-touch liberal who promoted homosexuality. Needless to say, Bush won the election by nearly eight percentage points.

While his defeat of Ann Richards was impressive, his reelection bid was stunning. He won 69% of the vote. Riding this wave of popularity and, some would claim, inspired by the Divine, Bush sought the office of U.S. President. Many candidates shy away from their religious affiliations, often viewing it as a liability. Bush made his spirituality a centerpiece of his campaign. Here was a man who prayed about important decisions and conversed in a manner that made him seem familiar to the average person. These qualities endeared him to evangelicals and conservatives. When Bush won the 2000 presidential electoral vote in one of the most controversial elections in history, the post-election analysis indicated that the evangelical and conservative blocks were the keys to his victory.

In 2004, Bush proved once again his understanding of the importance of defining the narrative. Despite a growing criticism of the Iraq war, he cast himself as the man most qualified and with the best track record for keeping the citizens of the United States safe. In a country still reeling from the terrorist attacks of September 11th, this narrative was immensely powerful. Bush defeated Democratic Senator John Kerry in a vote that needed no recount.

In that same year, George W. Bush's successor, Barack Obama, began laying out his own narrative that would elevate him to becoming the 44th President of the United States. A relative unknown, even among party insiders, Obama first arrived on the scene as a direct result of a well-received speech during the 2004 Democratic National Convention. Obama played to themes that resonate at the core of the American mythos. He opened the speech saying,

"Tonight is a particular honor for me because, let's face it, my presence on this stage is pretty unlikely. My father was a foreign student, born and raised in a small village in Kenya. He grew up herding goats, went to school in a tin-roof shack. His father, my grandfather, was a cook, a domestic servant to the British. But my grandfather had larger dreams for his son. Through hard work and perseverance, my father got a scholarship to study in a magical place, America, which shone as a beacon of freedom and opportunity to so many who had come before."

Later in the speech he would state,

"My parents shared not only an improbable love, they shared an abiding faith in the possibilities of this nation. They would give me an African name, Barack, or "blessed," believing that in a tolerant America your name is no barrier to success. They imagined me going to the best schools in the land even though they weren't rich because in a generous America you don't have to be rich to achieve your potential."

In a few short paragraphs, Obama had managed to invoke the values of hard work and perseverance, lauded the country as the land of opportunity, and even managed to sneak in a reference to a family history of indentured service to the British.

The reaction to his speech has become legendary: It launched his political career (like Bush, Obama actually lost his first U.S. Congressional election in 2000). Riding the momentum generated from the 2004 Convention, Obama won the election to represent Illinois in the Senate later that year. In four short years, he would defeat Hillary Clinton in the Democratic primaries (considered one of the greatest political upsets in recent years) and John McCain in the general election to become President of the United States. While Obama had certainly earned his fair share of admirers on that stage in Boston, few could have imagined they were looking at the next leader of the free world.

On his way to the highest office of the land, Obama consistently referenced strong American themes and his family's history. What he rarely mentioned was that he was the first black man who had a serious opportunity of winning a presidential election. For a nation that never had a nonwhite President, Vice President, or Speaker of the House, Obama was careful to downplay the significance of the color of his skin. Obama and his advisors accurately surmised concentrating their narrative on breaking the presidential color barrier was a losing formula. Only a select portion of the population would be intrigued with this notion, and just as many would be deterred. Instead, Obama focused more on the skills and perspective developed growing up in a multicultural home than on the unprecedented success of his campaign. He would argue that a man who grew up needing to bridge two cultures possessed the qualities necessary to bring together a nation tired of endless war and partisan bickering.

Obama's only real obstacle on his way to the presidency came when a tape involving his longtime pastor was leaked to the media. In this video capturing a sermon about September 11th, the Reverend Jeremiah Wright (a black man himself) provocatively discussed the relationship between black Americans and the country as a whole:

"The government gives them the drugs, builds bigger prisons, passes a three-strike law, and then wants us to sing 'God Bless America.' No, no, no! God damn America, that's in the Bible for killing innocent people. God damn America for treating our citizens as less than human."

The Reverend Wright had maintained close ties with Obama, presiding over his wedding and baptizing his children. This development shifted the narrative back to the color of Obama's skin and, worse, played on the fears of many that a black president would use his power to oppress the white majority.

Again, Obama used his considerable oratory aptitude to re-center his preferred storyline. In what is now known as the "race speech," Obama began by outlining the premise of equality outlined by the founding fathers. He legitimized the anger still reverberating in the essence of many African Americans by recognizing the promise of equality had been "stained" by the "original sin" of slavery. However, he quickly shifted the conversation back to a message of shared experience and unity. He stated:

"I chose to run for the presidency at this moment in history because I believe deeply that we cannot solve the challenges of our time unless we solve them together—unless we perfect our union by understanding that we may have different stories but we hold common hopes; that we may not look the same and we may not have come from the same place but we all want to move in the same direction—toward a better future for our children and our grandchildren."

Here was Obama, the bridge builder—a man who would strive for justice and a better life not only for the black man and woman but also for all citizens of a great nation. By reclaiming this narrative, Obama was able to cruise to victory, winning the election by nearly 200 electoral votes. Four years later, while not as dramatically impressive, Obama become the first Democratic President to win two elections with over 50% of the popular vote since Franklin D. Roosevelt.

Undoubtedly, the next President of the United States will construct a narrative that will appeal to the mood of the electorate. This narrative will focus on the prevailing issues of the day but remain steeped in the themes of Americana. These American themes have been in development long before there was an official United States, when it was simply referred to as the New World. John Winthrop, in the early 1600s, invoked the sermons of Jesus when he described the New World as "a city upon a hill" to his fellow Puritan travelers. Winthrop proclaimed that such a place must operate as an example of morality and prosperity for all those who look upon it as a beacon of hope. It has come to symbolize the responsibility borne upon the citizens of this nation to spread their message of freedom and liberty throughout the world. Indeed, John F. Kennedy and Ronald Reagan have borrowed this imagery as a means to define the greatness of the earth's most dominant society and to serve as a foundation for policies both domestic and foreign.

America has carefully crafted this narrative, and for many searching for new opportunities and independence, it has lived up to this mighty reputation. As more thoroughly discussed in previous chapters, however, this overemphasis on equal opportunity has turned disappointment in reaching a lofty ambition into a deeply felt personal failure for many in the 99% while ignoring the considerable genetic and environmental variables outside their control. In many cases, they are unable to recover from this self-inflicted wound.

Most damagingly, this narrative of superiority has also been appropriated as a rationale to inflict violence and suffering. The idea of "manifest destiny" drove the boundaries of the United States westward during the 1800s through the perceived blessings of a Divine force, much to the detriment of the indigenous peoples that found themselves in its path. Once this destiny had been achieved, the building of an infrastructure of a great nation was borne on the backs of African slaves, indentured servants, and the newly immigrated from Europe, China, and a potpourri of countries around the world.

This presents a central concern when it comes to the concept of defining a narrative. For a dominant narrative to succeed, it often kills off any competing narratives. A nation will go to great lengths to ensure that the themes most relevant to its way of life and future access to power will prevail. Take, for instance, the 19th and 20th century practice of placing Native American children in boarding schools. These young people were forcibly removed from their families and placed into environments that aggressively persuaded them to reject the teachings of their culture for the practices of the dominant society. One common observance at these schools was for classes to be taught in English. A student caught speaking in his native tongue often faced humiliating consequences. Such a response was to imply that the language learned from birth was somehow dirty and unfit for educational discourse. This restricting of language was paradoxical in nature as it defies the American narrative and constitutionally protected right of freedom of expression.

If the primary goal is to protect the prevailing narrative, then one of the most effective strategies for achievement of that objective is eliminating any language containing stories or themes that might prove contradictory. Evidence that this strategy is pervasive throughout the world is the recent finding of a study found in the magazine New Scientist. The author, Will Knight, recites a scientific claim that, "Half of all human languages will have disappeared by the end of the century as smaller societies are assimilated into national and global cultures." With the death of a language also comes the death of how the life narrative of the people and their ancestors are told. Finely woven tapestries of human existence are no longer accessible to modern cultures.

Certainly, the 99% could certainly be excused for not rallying for the preservation of languages of which they probably have never heard. The vast majority of the 99% are able to tell their stories in a native tongue likely to survive for centuries to come. What is of importance to the 99%, however, is how narratives can be constructed as a means of garnering power and that these dominant narratives are often used to subjugate competing storylines. The surprising fact is that the narrative being buried might actually be your own. Across the planet and in every society, there are individuals who take stock of their lives and have a sinking feeling. No longer are the promises of those above them in the power hierarchy satisfying. The narrative that by following the agenda of those in charge, it is their birthright to improve their lives as did their parents and previous generations, rings untrue.

The books of their lives have somehow been hijacked, and it feels as though someone else is writing the chapters. We are expected to behave in a manner that is reflective of our race or ethnicity. We are shackled by or falsely admired for our socioeconomic status. Our occupations and rate of pay are dictated by our sex chromosomes. We are told in order to achieve beauty, satisfaction, and longevity, we must purchase certain products. To be accepted by a group or organization, we must adhere to a set of beliefs and values that may clash with our own authenticity and sense of right and wrong. The end result: The 99% are losing authorship of their own narrative and are giving up a piece of their own personal power. Those who have gained control of the narrative in the marketplace of goods, services, relationships, and ideas—as exemplified by the stories from the political arena—are those who are finishing first in a race of their own creation.

While our narratives are being written by others, a vast file of documents is being compiled. In this file are numerous statistics that have come to define who we are as a people. Our GPA and SAT scores determine what colleges or universities we will attend. Our body mass index (BMI) informs us if we are underweight, normal, overweight, or obese. Our blood pressure rate, cholesterol level, and white blood cell count establish whether we qualify for certain insurance and what price we will pay. Our credit score is the gateway for purchasing homes and vehicles. The number of friends or admirers we have on social media websites indicates our relational prowess. These numbers, these snapshots in time, do not begin to encapsulate who we are as individuals. When numbers become our public persona and others are left to define our narrative (she's fat, he's lazy, she's dumb, he's unpopular), the qualities and achievements that make us who we are and lead to our own standard of satisfaction are buried. As Epston and White pointed out, it is important for all of us to maintain a counter-file that illuminates the positives inherent in each individual: a complimentary e-mail from a friend, a letter of recommendation from a supervisor, a touching card from a relative, a photo capturing a triumph or a fond memory.

Though I had been feeling it deep down inside for years, it took my encounters with Bob to realize that I was beginning to lose control of my own narrative. One of the prevalent themes of my narrative and that of my family was that education leads to opportunity. I had traveled across and lived in three continents to gain access to the finest universities and training. I made the United States my home because it offered the best chance for someone who lacked an establishment background to forge his own destiny. I wanted my children to be born in the United States so they could never be denied citizenship and the right to attend the best schools and select professions that mirrored their passion. In this regard and with considerable help from my wife, I was successful. However, in the process, I also began to accumulate possessions and other baggage that directly challenged what was important to me: the freedom of choice and never having to compromise my sense of decency. Instead, I was dependent on others and the income they provided me in order to sustain my current way of life.

Like the students at the charter school, it was time for me to recapture my narrative. When a narrative therapist works with a client to re-author his or her story, a set of questions is offered to help the individual challenge preconceived notions and construct new meaning. Anyone can ask oneself these questions. I find reflecting on them periodically an extremely useful exercise.

Below are a few of the questions paraphrased from Stephan Madigan's book, Narrative Therapy, and some answers to serve as examples.

Question: What does it mean to be a part of a certain society, culture, group, family unit?

Answer: Being a part of American society means access to resources and choices unthinkable when I was growing up in Pakistan.

Question: How does this ideology help you with the person you wish to be?

Answer: It allows me clear paths to the experiences, opportunities, and possessions that I find desirable.

Question: What are some potential pitfalls of aspiring to living this way?

Answer: It leads to a barrage of temptations and sets up an expectation that you must have certain things in order to maintain a preferred status.

Question: What might it mean for you to go against this ideology or way of thinking?

Answer: It could mean losing everything that I have gained or accumulated. It also could mean being freed of the anchor of always having to produce for someone else.

Question: Give an example of when you did operate against the grain.

Answer: Growing up and well into my 20s, I often had few articles of clothing, relied on public transportation, carried chump change in my pockets, and slept on floors. I would categorize it as one of the happier and more liberating periods of my life.

By engaging in this process, I was able to confront my fears about adopting a more humble lifestyle similar to the one of Bob, the social worker. My ultimate conclusion was that I had already experienced this approach and thus possessed the necessary skills and fortitude to achieve my objective. Similarly, many individuals have given up on an existence more akin to their dreams and to their authentic self because a predominant narrative makes them believe any alternative will be met with overwhelming difficulty. It becomes the proverbial swimming upstream, pushing a boulder up a steep hill, or walking into a gale-force wind. The perceived challenges and the subsequent fear are often more debilitating than warranted. Inside each individual is the capacity to reject what has been written for them and become the author of their own narrative.

To illustrate my final point about constructing one's own narrative, I want to bring you back to the school I described at the beginning of this chapter. For more than 20 years, one man has kept the building running with sheer guile and a whole lot of duct tape. His role as building manager isn't always glamorous, especially when he is called upon to clean bathrooms or repair heating units on the roof in -15° temperatures. He does each task, though, seriously and with a sense of humor to get him through the tough times; you know the job will get done right. All the students know him by name and genuinely like him. He takes pride in their growth and development. He has the work ethic, people skills, financial savvy, and resiliency that would make him a successful CEO of a company or executive director of a nonprofit. Approaching the age at which most people retire, he will likely have to delay this opportunity.

Growing up in the ghettos of Fort Wayne, Indiana probability dictated that he was most likely to be in a gang, deal drugs, live in perpetual poverty, or die young. He credits some timely mentors, in particular one of his aunts, as pivotal players in developing a strong resiliency and thus his ability to transcend this existence. Every now and then, he saddles up his well-tuned motorcycle and makes the 600-mile trip between his new home and his old home to attend the funeral of a family member or acquaintance. These individuals were unable to escape their circumstances. This climb out of poverty did not come without significant consequences: He was unable to garner the necessary resume of education and career experience necessary to receive the keys to the executive washroom.

This fact doesn't discourage him. He has taken the long view in a world constantly promoting immediate results and gratification. He has used his unique positioning (everyone needs the guy who can fix the air conditioning, plow the sidewalk, respond to a break-in, address a leaky ceiling, and repair all manner of furniture) to ensure a better quality of life for those around him. Most notably, he has provided the guidance and security for his own children to attend establishments of higher education. His two daughters and one son all have graduated from prestigious private universities and have parlayed this success into well-paying jobs with retirement and health insurance benefits—a scenario he could only imagine when he was in his 20s. With their college degrees, doors will be open for them that he could never walk through as a young man.

Early on, he rejected the prevailing narrative of impoverished black man and created the narrative of caretaker of young people's future. He is the living embodiment that narratives are cross-generational: They are passed down from grandparent to child to grandchild. When he sits and listens to the parents speak at the school's graduation of what this accomplishment means not only for their son or daughter but also for the family as a whole, he nods with approval and understanding.

Power Points

- *At-risk youth* are often defined by a *narrative* of misconduct, disengagement, and incompetence in school, leading to actions and beliefs that perpetuate a cycle of failure.

- N*arrative therapy* techniques can help take what are perceived to be weaknesses and *re-author* these qualities into skills needed for positive *transformation*.

- The elite are well aware of the importance of *controlling the narrative* and use considerable talent and resources to turn vulnerabilities into power sources.

- Societies emphasize the *narrative* that supports the dominant culture's values and themes while often devaluing less powerful subcultures.

- This approach has led to movements such as *Manifest Destiny* and *Language Extinction,* practices designed to snuff out *competing storylines* of rival ethnic traditions.

- Many individuals unwittingly give up their *narrative* and allow others to define who they are and how the chapters of their life will read.

- The 99% must reclaim a personal narrative that draws from examples of success and perseverance found in a *counter-file* that is centered on personal strengths and focuses on *cross-generational promotion*.

Next Destination

By examining our core commonalties, we can harness power from facing life's most pressing questions: why are we here and how do we address our pending mortality?

9

The Best of All Possible Worlds

Rule of the Road: Cultivate your garden.

Mile Markers: Terracotta Warriors, Immortality, Voltaire, The Best of All Possible Worlds, Higher Power, The Ten Commandments, Spirituality, Secular Migration, Dalai Lama, Golden Rule, Atheism, War Audit, Universal Values, Legacy

My wife of more than 40 years has long claimed that I suffer from wanderlust. I suppose the evidence favors her appraisal. Before the age of 35, I had called home some of the largest cities in the world: New Delhi, Karachi, London, Montreal, and New York. Since then, my professional career has afforded me the opportunity to visit every habitable continent and experience the lifestyles in scores of different countries. While I can appreciate these cultures' distinctive food, clothing, practices, and traditions, I have been struck more by what makes us similar than what sets us apart. In particular, the needs that are deemed essential, the desires we share, and the questions we meditate on are all a part of the universal human fabric. Whether it is of a social worker in a small, rural hospital or an administrator of one the major medical centers in the country; whether it is an at-risk adolescent attending a charter school in an impoverished urban neighborhood or a world class athlete attending an iconic sport's high school; or whether it is a child living in the rubble of a war-torn Sarajevo or a lottery winner basking in the glow of new-found wealth; our commonalities cannot be denied.

It is my belief that examining these commonalities, mining them down to their core elements, is critical in the process of taking control of the direction of our narrative and harnessing a power that will sustain us through the numerous challenges we face on this earth. Of course, I am not remotely the first person to expend mental capital on this topic. On a recent trip to visit my youngest son and his family, I was reminded in spectacular fashion that this human condition, what we struggle and strive for, has spanned countless generations.

Like many of our most thought provoking experiences, it started off modestly: My son had scored four tickets to attend a special exhibit centered on the world-renowned Terracotta Warriors of China. While expecting a fulfilling couple of hours, what I encountered in these enclosed rooms both fascinated me on a visceral level and challenged my concept of what I had perceived to be the limits of power and wealth.

The exhibit contained examples of a vast army of life-sized, stone warriors complete with armor, chariots, and horses, dating back to the year 210 BC. Fixated by their carved eyes, I couldn't help but reflect on my own ancestry, as if I were staring at my forefathers from the Mongol portion of my family tree. Of the over 7,000 warriors so far discovered, no two are exactly alike. Today's master artisans would be hard-pressed to undertake such an endeavor even with the advancements of material and technique of the last 2,000 years. The man behind this extravaganza demanded absolute perfection. His name was Qin Shi Huang. The question that resonated with me long after I left the museum was: What would possess this mortal to push the boundaries of human ability and capacity to such an extreme?

To understand his motivations, it was important for me to examine the context in which he lived. China at the time was made up of several states that were at constant war. At the age of 13, Qin was named the emperor of the Chi state. In a sign of the volatile era, his predecessor had only occupied the throne for three years. Chi was considered insignificant by some of the other more influential states. It had the reputation of being barbaric and unsophisticated. This might explain why it had become increasingly more powerful while virtually unnoticed. Reportedly leading his well-armed troops into battle, Qin Shi Huang would conquer the other warring states and unify them under one dynasty, earning himself the distinction of

China's first emperor at the age of 34. In 21 short years, he would bring the end to a millennium of feudal war that had dominated China.

With his unprecedented power, Qin developed a ruling style that was both brilliant and ruthless. Brilliant in the sense that he connected a series of fortified barriers that became known as the Great Wall of China to limit the constant bombardment of invaders from the north. He created a uniform money system that previously had several forms of coins and currency types, simplifying financial transactions. He standardized the roads and strung across the landscape several canals to ease and increase the speed of travel through his newly unified empire. He was ruthless in the sense that he instituted a series of rules and consequences intended to keep his rivals precariously positioned under his boot. Punishments were designed to intensify suffering in the offenders and strike fear in those who may consider challenging his unquestioned authority. Not even his own family members were spared his bloodshed.

Almost immediately after ascending the throne, Qin began to attend to his afterlife with the same ferocity with which he approached the here and now. Every detail was painstakingly managed to ensure a successful transition upon death, including the placement of the burial mound in a direct line to China's most scared mountains. Thousands of stone suits of armor were placed in a pit for the souls of his warriors who had fallen in battle and would presumably continue their fight in the next world. He would employ over 700,000 skilled laborers to accomplish this task and the other components of his mausoleum. In many cases, these individuals' lives were devoted to this solitary cause.

While touring the empire he created just shy of his 50th birthday, Qin Shi Huang would afford himself the opportunity to test their meticulous preparations. Qin fell ill and died. His body was transported to his tomb per his instructions. With one last act of megalomania and paranoia, hundreds of his concubines and many of his workers with intimate knowledge of the tomb's contents were sealed behind the thick doors with their emperor to share his fate.

Qin Shi Huang was a ruler of unparalleled drive and resources. He was obsessed, however, with the same question or fear that mystifies all human beings: What will happen to me once my time on earth is done? Despite his superior status, he was plagued with the problem of addressing his impending mortality. This subject, regardless of our accomplishments, hangs over each of us with equal urgency. It is a tie that binds us all together.

Seventeen hundred years later, a noted French philosopher would write a book about another central theme that unites humanity. The story, which still remains a curriculum staple for numerous school systems in the Western world, focuses on a young man's travels. The author's name was Voltaire, and the book was Candide.[53]

Born in 1694 during a time in France when the aristocracy was still in its prime, the seeds of democratic change would begin to take root during Voltaire's considerable lifetime. While he would die a decade before the storming of the Bastille, his ideas of religious tolerance and a government working for the people were key in forming the justification for the French Revolution.[54]

Voltaire's life would span the reigns of Louis XIV, Louis XV, and the famously executed Louis XVI. It was a time when power and wealth were strongly concentrated in an elite few. This inequitable distribution would lead Voltaire to write extensively about the three estates of the clergy, the nobles, and the large majority of the population, the commoners. The last and biggest of these groups held little influence, were suffocated by financial obligations to the monarchy, and endured difficult working conditions with little opportunity for advancement. They were subject to the whims of established classes without any political representation. However, in comparison to the poor (so powerless as to be ignored by Voltaire's examination of the three estates), the commoners had the "good life." The poor of France overcrowded the streets and fought daily against the threats of hunger and disease.

Against this backdrop, a young Voltaire surrounded himself with other writers who used various pen-and-ink genres to satirize the political and noble scene surrounding them. According to the *Stanford Encyclopedia of Philosophy*[55], Voltaire embraced the role of radical intellectual despite being born into and extremely connected to French high society. His opinions led him to exile from both France and Germany for periods of time and his writings prompted officials to order their burning. Fashioning himself as an insurgent among the elite, he saw himself as uniquely positioned to drag France out of the darkness of previous thinking and into the enlightenment

---

53   English translation available at http://www.gutenberg.org/ebooks/19942

54   While considered a strong influence among the faction for both the American and French Revolution, even having close ties with Benjamin Franklin, Voltaire was leery of democracy. He lamented that most individuals lacked the mental capacity and necessary education to elect effective leaders.

55   *Stanford Encyclopedia of Philosophy*. Voltaire. August 31, 2009. Retrieved October 30, 2014 from http://plato.stanford.edu/entries/voltaire/

of scientific thought. Taking such a position caused him to have many de-tractors and he would spend much of his career defending his arguments while attacking, with vigor, those with whom he disagreed.

Chief among his targets was the popular philosopher Leibniz. Leibniz was already 48 in the year Voltaire was born and would be dead before his rival would publish a meaningful work. Today, Leibniz is probably better known for his contributions to mathematics as his theories and findings are still being built upon in fields as diverse as calculus and computer pro-gramming. At that time, Leibniz's philosophical influence was wide-reach-ing in France and other parts of Europe. Since his thinking represented the more accepted and traditional view, the insurgent Voltaire would need to confront Leibniz's ideas with great gusto to legitimize his own philosophy.

In his book Théodicée[56], Leibniz deduced that we live in "the best of all possible worlds." He reasoned that, since God was perfect, the world around us is the optimum outcome of an infinite number of outcomes. Surrounded by disease, famine, and poverty, inundated with natural di-saster that killed the innocent and downtrodden at greater rates than the affluent and culpable, Voltaire found this conclusion both laughable and dangerous.

For a man skeptical of religion and an advocate of scientific reasoning, Leibniz's writings on "optimism" would prove to be the most advantageous battleground for Voltaire. Further, he would use his seminal work Candide as a powerful weapon. For those of you who struggle to remember the finer points of 11th grade English, let me provide a brief synopsis of this classic and brutal satire: As the illegitimate relative of a well-positioned noble, Candide enjoys the protected and cozy life of the rich. That is, until he overreaches his social status and secretly courts Cunégonde, the beautiful daughter of a nobleman. When discovered, he is thrown out of the castle and into the unpredictable land of the commoner.

Accompanying him in his exile is his lifelong teacher, Dr. Pangloss. Pangloss envisions himself as an important philosopher, and he subscribes to the Leibniz belief that they live in "the best of all possible worlds." This personal mantra would face the ultimate test. During their epic travels, Candide and Pangloss endure ridicule, war, near-drowning, extreme hun-ger, floggings, and even a bout of syphilis. They bear witness to or commit murder, rape, and cannibalism. They manage to discover a fortune in dia-monds and proceed to lose almost all of it. When Candide and Cunégonde are finally reunited, Voltaire's seemingly fairytale conclusion adds insult to

---

56   English translation available at http://www.gutenberg.org/ebooks/17147

injury. Cunégonde's attractiveness has completely eroded to the point of hideousness.

Confronting overwhelming evidence to the contrary[57], Pangloss maintains his conviction that a society capable of such cruelty is still "the best of all possible worlds." Candide, on the other hand, no longer sides with the philosophy of his mentor. Jaded by his experiences, Candide simply wants to find some semblance of happiness. With his remaining precious gems, Candide purchases a home in the country and invites his fellow travelers who have survived this ordeal to live with him. Emotionally scarred and physically worn down by their encounters, the group manages to finally find peace and harmony by working the farmland surrounding the home. In summarizing this action, Candide utters the famous words "we must cultivate our garden," a phrase that still survives in the lexicon of today and a power-laden metaphor that will play an important role in the conclusion of this chapter.

Millennia apart and separated by the vastness of earth's largest continent, Voltaire and Qin Shi Huang would share a commonality in confronting the two questions quintessential to the human experience:

1) How do I best survive, find happiness, and leave my mark in a world that is often unpredictable, unfair, and full of suffering?

2) How do I prepare for my impending death and the potential life thereafter?

Regardless of our power and status in society or the strength of our intellect, these are the driving motivators of every human being who has walked this planet. This forethought serves as a critical divergence of humans from our animal brethren. Quality of life is an evaluation we make daily, and mortality extends beyond simple instincts to survive.

An examination of history demonstrates that as individuals formed groups and groups became communities, cultures independent of one another arrived at a similar conclusion to these questions. Humans would need a set of rules or guidelines in order for societies to thrive. Further, these sets of rules or guidelines would garner more influence if they were inspired and enforced by divine entities. Pleasing these omnipotent, omnipresent entities through obedience to these principles would lead to rewards in life and after death.

The Ten Commandments is one of the most well-known examples of this closed loop. Moses descends the same mountain where God first

---

57 In a plot twist worthy of Stephen King, Pangloss is hanged for blasphemy, presumed dead, and revealed to be alive only when a surgeon awakens him while cutting into his body.

spoke to him about freeing the Jewish slaves from the pharaoh with a set of rules for all His believers to follow. He finds "God's people" engaging in all sorts of debauchery, which humans are prone to do when left unsupervised. Sensing what we educators like to refer to as a "teachable moment," Moses chastises the descendants of Abraham for their actions and unfolds God's revelation in the form of the Ten Commandments. While seemingly simple by today's standards, they are a marvel in that modern societies regard these concepts as a given: Thou shall not kill, thou shall not steal, thou shall not commit adultery, thou shall not bear false witness, thou shall not covet thy neighbor's house, and thou shall honor thy father and mother. If it were openly permissible and expected for individuals to kill, steal, commit adultery, bear false witness, and disregard the authority of our parents, then how could any community function? There would be no sense of safety and no sense of protection, which would lead to perpetual conflict. Frankly, that was the baseline experience of most of our early ancestors.

Now, imagine if Moses had walked down the hill without the backing of the Divine and said, "Guys, I have had some time to meditate, and I came up with some really good stuff about how we should live our lives."

The Jews might say, "He is a pretty good guy; he did get us out of that jam. But Moses is just a man, and men die. Eventually, another man will take his place."

In contrast, God is immortal. It was God who brought the plagues of locusts and frogs. It was God who had the power to take away or spare our firstborn sons. It was God who did the impossible and parted the Red Sea. God reminds His people of this fact in the preamble of the Commandments by stating, "I am the LORD your God, who brought you out of the land of Egypt, out of the house of slavery." Seems like a pretty compelling case, doesn't it?

The most intriguing part is the purposes of the remaining Commandments: Thou shalt not have no other gods before me, thou shall not make unto thee any graven image, thou shall not take the name of thy God in vain, and remember the Sabbath day. In essence, God is instructing the Jews to adhere to some sensible rules, to respect the omnipotent deity that provided these rules, and to refrain from seeking other gods that might say differently. The last part is relevant because in the short time Moses was up the mountain, the masses had already begun to create and worship idols. In the creation of the Ten Commandments, God had thought of every angle and created an airtight cognitive construct. That's why He is God.

Before walking too far down this path, it is important to provide a moment of clarity. In establishment of rules, guidelines, ethics, and the linkage to a higher power, there are two general camps. The first camp believes that a higher power(s) has communicated to man and woman values to which each individual should aspire. In essence, a godlike figure or figures occasionally intervene to help us find a way of life that would greater ensure prosperity among the chosen people. Think Moses descending from Mount Sinai with the Ten Commandments. The other camp believes that, through the need to both establish order among the chaos and to come to terms with our mortality, deities emerged as a natural byproduct. To put it simply, Camp 1 states that God created humans and morality. Camp 2 states that humans created God and attributed morality to him. In the spirit of full disclosure, I am a member of Camp 1. As a devout Muslim and reinforced through my life experiences, it is the lens through which I view the world. Further, as a mental health practitioner, I can attest to the therapeutic impact of spirituality, faith, and religion in some of the darkest places in the world. As discussed more thoroughly in Chapter 7, few places in the past few decades have been as dark as Bosnia during my visits in the early '90s.

Among the Bosnian children with whom I worked was a 7-year-old boy who told a short story I will never forget. In front of a captivated and somber audience he said, "I don't understand this. Last year my neighbor gave me a birthday gift. I used to call him 'Uncle.' Two months ago he came with other men and killed my father and my older brother. I don't understand why." Certainly, this child would have a hard time accepting the Leibniz claim that we live in the best of all possible worlds. Where are this young boy, the estimated 10,000 children in New York who tragically lost a loved one on September 11, 2001, and the million more youth worldwide who are orphaned or separated from their parents due to war supposed to turn for solace?

One possible answer can be found in the safety, stability, and warmth associated with the belief in God or a higher power. This conviction has empowered many to overcome otherwise suffocating calamities. Research demonstrates that children who face trauma and have a mature faith are capable of harnessing a spiritual strength. For these children, their faith becomes an important resiliency factor for eventual recovery. As part of the healing process, they often need a reason to forgive the perpetrator and even sometimes themselves. Their relationship with God and the subsequent religious teachings can provide this opportunity. With resiliency and forgiveness as a foundation, victims of traumatic events are positioned to reclaim their narrative: The source of anger, disillusionment, and sadness is reframed as a deep well of strength and bravery that can always be drawn upon.

What has deepened my allegiance to Camp 1 is seeing the boy who lost his father and older brother transform from a lost and confused casualty to a survivor with resolve and purpose in part due to his religious practices. Further developing this fidelity is the fact that my spiritual connection to my God addresses the same questions surrounding the challenges of achieving one's life purpose that inspired Voltaire to write Candide while providing a hopeful path to the uncertainties of mortality that contrast with the madness that drove Qin Shi Huang to build his expansive mausoleum. The modern trend, however, has been decidedly the reverse. While not willing to go so far as to say they are members of Camp 2—rejection of the existence of God or higher power, many have drifted from their faith roots and traditions. In fact, the evidence of this secular migration is staggering.

A recent Pew study reports that one in five American adults has no specific affiliations to a religious organization.[58] Even faith-based schools, once a staple in almost every American city, have seen diminishing enrollments and the boarding up of windows. According to the numbers provided by archdioceses across the country, 26% of all Catholic schools have closed in the last decade. World trends also reflect a decline in religious affiliation. A Gallup poll of 57 countries revealed that only 59% of the world's population considers themselves religious.[59] That's a drop of 9% in just seven years when the survey was last completed.

In an interview with ABC News[60] about the earlier study, Robert Putnam attributes this decline to a belief that religions foster "intolerance and rigidity and doctrinaire political views." Such characterization will do poorly among the millennials, who are ever more interconnected and have regular exposure to different upbringings and backgrounds. Religions also have deep associations in the minds of many that are the antithesis of their

---

58   Pew Research Center's Forum on Religion & Public Life. *"Nones" on the Rise: One-in-Five-Adults Have No Religious Affiliation.* October 9, 2012. Retrieved October 30, 2014 from http://www.pewforum.org/files/2012/10/NonesOnTheRise-full.pdf

59   WIN-Gallup International. Global Index of Religiosity and Atheism, 2012. Retrieved October 30, 2014 from http://www.wingia.com/web/files/news/14/file/14.pdf

60   Harris D. Young Americans Losing Their Religion, New Research Finds Number Who Claim No Church Has Risen Sharply. May 6, 2009. Retrieved October 30, 2014 from http://abcnews.go.com/Politics/print?id=7513343

stated purposes: Harmony is replaced with conflict, love is replaced by hate, safety is replaced by fear, trust is displaced by dishonesty, and most prominently, peace is replaced by war.

The Gallup poll independently reinforces Putnam's claims as countries that have experienced systemic corruption or scandal among their religious entities have suffered the steepest decline in religious participation. Most notably, the country of Ireland, synonymous with all things Catholic, saw such a challenge to this foundation that it might take the resurrection of St. Patrick himself to lead a revival. He will have an easier time using the clover leaf to explain the Holy Trinity or driving the unwanted snakes out of the homeland than he will bringing people back to the Church if the clergy continue to be mired in accusations of child sexual abuse. During the height and fallout of this crisis, the number of Irish individuals identifying as religious plunged from 69% to 47%.

The recent Irish experience is certainly not an outlier. Every decade of the 20th century is riddled with conflicts with perceived undertones of religious strife and destruction. Each century of recorded history speaks to these same themes. Take, for example, the two prominent subjects of this chapter. Qin Shi Huang was able to justify not only his wanton destruction of the rival Kingdoms of China but also the murder of those whose entire lives were devoted to the preservation of his legacy because such was the will of the gods. Only when it seemed that the "heavens" had withdrawn support of Huang were his detractors able to garner enough resolve to end his tyrannical reign.

Voltaire, observing the atrocities of his day, reserved his most strident criticism for the clergy. In Candide, the Church is the perpetrator of nearly every imaginable crime: execution of those who espouse a different belief, beating people for merely being in the same area as individuals espousing a different belief, stealing precious items, indifference to the suffering around them, and the wanton breaking of celibacy vows. Such is the level of controversy that even Dan Brown of Da Vinci Code fame would likely steer clear of the Voltairian portrayal of clergy keeping gay lovers and popes openly fathering daughters. In a move reminiscent of a Tarantinoesque revenge fetish, Voltaire has Candide violently kill the Grand Inquisitor since he served as the embodiment of all Church corruption.

While this phenomenon of religious exploitation and the subsequent satirical response is not remotely new, what has changed is that the examples are more prominently on display for a mass audience to consume through multiple media sources. We are privy to the pictures and stories of Bosnian Muslim women and children forced into makeshift prisons referred to as "rape camps" at the hands of Serbian Orthodox Christians. One can hardly turn on the television without hearing about the ongoing turmoil and failed peace attempts between the Israelis and the Palestinian Authority.

Even the Buddhist, considered the standard bearer of nonviolence, has been marked by aggressive action recently. In Burma, a series of coordinated attacks by Buddhist monks on Muslim homes and mosques have left hundreds dead and many injured. Most visibly, terrorism has become synonymous with Islamic fundamentalism because of the religiously motivated attacks on some of the Western World's largest cities—London, Madrid, New York, Boston, and Paris. The deplorable and ruthless acts of the Islamic State of Iraq and Syria (ISIS) have hijacked the belief system of 1.5 billion people and left the rest of the planet wondering if Islam promotes hate and destruction.

These events have all occurred in the last 25 years. Is it surprising that as a collective society we may be suffering from some "God fatigue" as our perception surrounding organized religion becomes tarnished and possibly hostile? Isn't it a positive development that we increasingly hold our religious leaders accountable while viewing religious entities with an eye of skepticism?

The answers contain qualities of both "Yes" and "No." Yes, in the sense that religious leaders must be held to the highest standards because they represent a code of ethics passed down from our Creator. No, in that accompanying this collective cynicism is the erosion of something essential: the personal investment in the code of ethics our leaders are attempting to ascribe. Most alarmingly, this diminished ethical center begins to fray the "ties that bind" all societies and all walks of life.

Don't take it from me; read about it directly from a man who has spent every breath of his life exploring these themes.[61] The Dalai Lama is the spiritual leader of Tibet and is considered to be an enlightened being of compassion. He often speaks of what he defines as the "present worldwide moral crisis." The prevailing wisdom of the day is to focus on the anger and hatred that arises from the differences in religion. This modern approach lends itself to a culture more inclined not only to reject religion but also to be left with the default setting of believing in nothing. The Dalai Lama views this conclusion as especially dangerous and instead stresses the importance of examining the interconnection of all faiths. This bond

---

61   Buddhists would argue that, since he is the incarnation of previous Dalai Lamas, not
      only has he spent his life but the lives of 13 predecessors pondering these questions.

centers upon compassion, love, and the overall benefit of humanity: "All religions teach moral precepts for perfecting the functions of mind, body, and speech." Through this process we learn not to lie, not to cheat, to treat people fairly, and to practice unselfishness.

The Dalai Lama emphasizes the quest to deem one religion as superior is fruitless. On the contrary, everyone should embrace the common message permeating all religions. "Humanity needs all the world's religions to suit its ways of life: diverse spiritual needs and inherited national traditions of individual human beings." Further, "each religion has its own distinctive contributions to make, and each, in its own way, is suitable to a particular group of people as they understand life. The world needs them all."

If the focus is shifted from the specific rituals and theologies to a values orientation, then it is possible to find a consensus pathway to human happiness. One clear example of these common values is taught to all children and is aptly termed "The Golden Rule." Below are the platitudes and scripture of Christian, Buddhist, Hindu, Islamic, and Jewish faith regarding the Golden Rule[62]:

Christianity:
"Therefore all things whatsoever ye would that men should do to you, do ye even so to them: For this is the law and the prophets" (Matthew 7:12).
"Thou shalt love thy neighbor as thyself. On these two commandments hang all the law and the prophets" (Matthew 22:39–40).

Buddhism:
Bahaiullah said, "Blessed is he who prefereth his brother before himself" and "O kings of the earth! ... Do not rob them [the people] to rear palaces for yourselves; nay rather choose for them that which ye choose for yourselves. Thus we unfold to your eyes that

---

62   All verses were taken from the sacred texts from each religion; however, they were expertly compiled by Dr. Christopher Buck for his article, "Religions Share Enduring Values," available at http://bahai-library.com/buck_abc-clio_enduring_values. A fascinating article, he also examines other religions' versions of the "Golden Rule" not listed above.

which profiteths you, if ye but perceive. Your people are your treasures ... By them ye rule, by their means ye subsist, by their aid ye conquer."

Hinduism:
"I shall tell thee what constitutes as the highest good of a human being ... He who regards all creatures as his own self and behaves towards them as his own self, laying aside the rod of chastisement and completely subjugating his wrath, succeeds in attainment to happiness. The very deities who are desirous of a fixed abode become stupefied in ascertaining the track of that person who constitutes himself the soul of all creatures and looks upon him all as his own self, for such a person leaves no track behind. One should never do to another what one regards as injurious to one's own self. This in brief is the rule of righteousness" (Mahabharata 13.113.6–9).

Islam:
The Prophet Muhammad said, "Whoever wishes to be delivered from the fire and enter the garden should with faith in Allah and the last day and should treat the people as he wishes to be treated by them," and *"None of you [truly] believes until he wishes for his brother what he wishes for himself." [official English translation of the Qur'anic verse]*

Judaism:
"Thou shalt not take vengeance, nor bear any grudge against the children of thy people, but thou shalt love thy neighbor as thyself: I am the LORD" (Leviticus 19:18).

Take a moment to read these texts again. They are astonishingly similar. Not to mistake my next statement for heresy, but you could mix and match the various verses with the different religions and never be the wiser (once you account for religion-specific terms such as Allah). Christians take communion, Muslims pray five times a day, Hindus focus on meditation, Jews observe the Sabbath, and Buddhists incorporate a prayer wheel. The "Golden Rule" is one of many proofs that religions may have many foreign-looking vehicles but are ultimately traveling the same road to the same destination.

Some find it challenging that "nonbelievers" often arrive at this destination as well. An atheist is someone who rejects the existence of a higher power (the antonym of atheism is theism, the belief in God(s)). Like any group of people subscribing to a worldview, atheists come in all shapes and sizes. However, what really gets most atheists' dander up is the assumption that disavowing God subsequently leads to a lack of a moral code. Atheist and writer Adam Lee writes prolifically on this topic. By espousing rational thought and scientific method as his compass in the article, "We Don't Need Religion to Have Morality,"[63] he comes to the following conclusion: "If your success is others' success as well, they'll have every reason to work with you and assist you, rather than opposing you and impeding you from achieving your goals. Regardless of what you personally desire, the best thing for you is to live in a society that values honesty, generosity, fairness, and the like." Sounds like the foundation for an atheist version of the Golden Rule.

In essence, Lee's argument falls under the Camp 2 scenario described earlier. It is the belief people will naturally come to the conclusion that a society that promotes universally accepted values will likely lead to more advancement for all. The need for a god, in their eyes, is unnecessary. In fact, it can be counterproductive. Lee argues in a corollary article, "The Basis for an Atheist's Morality,"[64] that religion equally giveth and taketh away. Lee concedes religion has "... inspired great acts of charity and selflessness ... " but has also been the impetus for " ... countless incidents of discrimination, prejudice, and bigotry." He writes, "Far from being a force that pulls ceaselessly toward the moral apex of the universe, religion is more like a

---

63   Lee D. We Don't Need Religion to Have Morality. September 14, 2011. Retrieved October 30, 2014 from http://www.patheos.com/blogs/daylightatheism/2011/09/religion-and-morality/

64   Lee D. The Basis for an Atheist's Morality. July 14, 2007. Retrieved October 30, 2014 from http://www.patheos.com/blogs/daylightatheism/2007/07/basis-for-an-atheists-morality/

megaphone, amplifying both the good and the bad of human nature in equal measure."

Most atheists and theists would generally agree with two of Lee's major assertions:

All beings should strive for a world that is copassionate and just for the betterment of all humans.

Acts of oppression and cruelty under the guise or protection of religion are a chief culprit in diminishing this harmony.

Instead of centering on the shared message, however, we fall victim to the trap of obsessing on how we reached these conclusions. "My God is better than your God" or "No God is better than any God" becomes the mantra of individuals entrenched in a hole they have dug themselves into and refuse to climb out of. Bickering and infighting cause us to lose hold of the significance of our commonalities.

The end result is that it has become easy, almost customary, to blame religion for humanity's shortcomings and violent atrocities. Call it an over-correction induced by outrage. An examination of history's most brutal and deadly conflicts demonstrates that there is plenty of fault to go around. Charles Phillips and Alan Axelrod, in Encyclopedia of Wars[65], take an extensive approach to the issue, investigating 1,763 wars throughout time. Their conclusions mirror my central point: A sparse 7% are determined to be religious in nature. Austin, Kranock, and Oommen summarized these surprising findings with the following declaration, "At a philosophical level, the main religious traditions have little truck with war or violence. All advocate peace as the norm and see genuine spirituality as involving a disavowal of violence. It is mainly when organized religious institutions become involved with state institutions or when a political opposition is trying to take power that people begin advocating religious justifications for war." Religion has long been the cover for people and nations to legitimize their personal agendas and eventual power grabs.

This study is a reminder that while we are armed with a slew of information and unfettered access to the faults of our faith institutions, we must be careful that, in our distaste for the perceived actions of religious entities, we avoid falling victim to the proverbial "throwing the baby out with the bathwater." Yes, the bathwater is cloudy and has been dirtied by the imperfections of humanity. In the baby, though, we have a set of ethical convictions and a subsequent value system that Muslims, Jews, Christians,

---

65   Phillips C, Axelrod A. *Encyclopedia of Wars*. Three-volume set. New York: Facts on File, 2004.

Buddhists, Hindus, other faith traditions, and atheists all promote and ascribe to. In that universal truth, in these ties that bind, there exists access to an unlimited source of personal power.

To find the location of this power source, we must return to the garden, the final chapter of Candide's saga and a place of significant religious and spiritual symbolism. For the Abrahamic religions, the garden (of Eden) is the representation of perfection and paradise. It is where all God's creatures roamed in absolute comfort and without need. It is also a reminder of man's and woman's fall from grace, serving as a contrast to the hardships and difficulties plaguing the human existence. For Buddhists, the garden is ideal for meditation and reflection. Many Buddhist temples have adjacent, well-manicured gardens to promote spiritual awakening. In the Hindu oral tradition, a garden is a sanctuary where a worshiper might find one of the over 300,000,000 forms of Brahma (the Supreme God) at play.

Similarly, Voltaire's garden is a refuge for Candide and his fellow travelers from the atrocities both inflicted on and performed by them in a cruel world. However, Voltaire's garden deviates from the harmonious, carefree narrative that dominates the motifs of most faith traditions. In his garden, inhabitants must toil away to reap any benefits from the land. Through this intense labor, a sense of peace can be obtained. Before anyone jumps to the conclusion that Voltaire is advocating a deep-rooted American theme—a strong work ethic leads to prosperity, it is important to note his true underlying message. Without the daily routine of cultivating your own garden, the mind is left to speculate on the happenings of the environment around it. These ruminations can develop into convictions, and convictions can lead to broadly followed schools of philosophy that Voltaire deemed dangerous.

Remember, Voltaire was openly challenging the widely-held belief of optimism prevailing in the elite of his time. He considered this unfounded optimism a disturbing worldview because of the throngs of indigent and poor people across the European landscape. Left with the choice of either denying the multitude of societal injustices or attempting to come to terms with the vagrancies of unpredictable and often callous surroundings, Voltaire prescribes a third choice: Deal with what is immediately in front of you. As any farmer or weekend gardener will tell you, cultivating the land keeps you grounded and offers little opportunity to ponder anything else but the task at hand. It is almost a coda to the saying, "idle hands are the devil's workshop," whose origins are attributed to Voltaire's literary predecessor, Geoffrey Chaucer.

These models of a garden, while instructive for where we have been, provide only limited guidance for a modern and interconnected world. A new garden paradigm must be created if we are ever to inspire humanity to embody the principles and morals common to all cultures, societies, and religions. The agreed-upon values of compassion, integrity, service, and responsibility will provide the framework to build these enlightened grounds. To this end, the 21st century version of a garden can neither be a utopian paradise that we long to discover nor a refuge from the harsh realities of the world. On the contrary, the garden must hold a place in everyday life and be in full view for everyone to see. The gardens cannot be reserved to sacred temples but must exist in the homes, schools, and work areas of every human being.

The garden of today must be devoid of 10-foot stone walls designed to restrict admittance only to the owners. Instead, welcome signs should be posted and guests treated with honor. For the modern garden to thrive, caretakers must willingly want to share the fruits of their labors with their neighbors, constituency, and passersby. In turn, the same caretakers would feel free to respectfully enter and appreciate the splendor of the other gardens around them. Collectively, they would represent what is best about a community and demonstrate the diversity of aptitude that lies within.

While communal in nature, the modern garden must also be the showcase for individual talent. The talent may be artistic in nature such as painting, music, dance, and poetry. Think of the man who engages children to paint a mural celebrating the diversity of their community. The talent may be pragmatic such as carpentry, handling machinery, and peacekeeping. Think of the woman who uses the workbench in her garage to repair her snow blower so she can clear the sidewalks and driveways of the elderly in her neighborhood. The talent may be social welfare or academic in practice, like scientific study, policy-making, and teaching. Think of the couple who spearheads a clothing and food drive for the needy in their area. Whatever the case, we must fill the spaces we inhabit with the skills that we have been given and those that have been nurtured within us.

As I did in previously challenging you regarding your personal narrative, take a moment to imagine how your garden would look. Built from the materials of your life, what would you hope it would contain? How would the act of "cultivating your own garden" promote your happiness and that of those around you? Envision a society where everyone demonstrates personal ownership of his or her garden by taking pride in its upkeep and striving for the creation of beauty in areas that were once barren.

Such an approach would go a long way in addressing the two fundamental questions of human existence broached in the beginning of this chapter—how to navigate and achieve happiness in an often difficult and unfair world and how to come to terms with our impending mortality. Maintaining a personal garden enables each individual to avoid being washed away by the tide of bad news and tragedy. It provides a manageable goal in the sense that no one person must solve a multitude of overwhelming problems. Instead, we simply focus on the piece of the puzzle within our reach. The modern garden provides an avenue to showcase our talents. It is a source of satisfaction where others can share in our gifts, knowing that we have assisted our fellow human being. The concept of open gardens assures us that, in our eventual moment of need, we may benefit from the hard work and skill of another.

Finally, a properly cultivated garden will last well beyond the time when our bodies are laid to rest. Our garden represents the legacy of our time here on earth. Qin Shi Huang had this strategy of immortality in mind when he constructed his imposing garden. With the unification of a country and the subsequent untold resources at his disposal, Qin had a unique historical opportunity to create a garden that would have greatly enriched the lives of his people. Instead, his garden ignored core ethical principles and was alternatively built out of fear, greed, narcissism, and oppression. In his need to live forever, he overlooked the idea that memories live on in the hearts of the people we have loved; our achievements are passed on in the deeds of those whom we have nurtured and for whom we have cared.

The price for his miscalculation was heavy. Poisoned by his own advisors and his corpse covered with rotting fish to hide his death, Qin's life came to an unceremonious end. Though his wish of being entombed in his magnificent mausoleum was granted, the grandeur of this burial would be fleeting. The kingdom he had ruled with an iron fist was conquered less than five years after his death. The palace he built for his afterlife lay in ruins and was lost for millennia. Indeed, the very weapons that were forged by his skilled artisans and furnished for the Terracotta Warriors were appropriated by the factions who eventually overthrew Qin's fledging dynasty. The outer parts of his tomb were burned, and many of the Terracotta Warriors designed to protect him were broken into pieces by his many enemies. Even his eldest son, his personally chosen heir apparent, was tricked into committing suicide.

Qin Shi Huang's legacy is a reminder that we can spend the capital of our power in the pursuit of accumulating a mausoleum of treasures. At the end of our lives, we can't take a single item with us. Instead, we should consider planting our garden, however modest, and have our grandchildren watch it grow long after our time in this world has passed.

Power Points

- Regardless of culture or time period, human beings have been searching for answers to two quintessential questions: how do I make the most out of my life and how do I come to terms with my *mortality*?

- To help address these questions, societies developed a framework of ethics and laws, attributed to a deity or *higher power*(s), that would lead to rewards both in life and after death.

- Belief in a higher power and a deep rooted *spirituality* has allowed countless people to overcome the stress, anxiety, and mental illness that accompany life's tragedies.

- Despite the noted benefits of spirituality, more individuals are turning to a *secular* lifestyle as the world religions are mired in controversy and increased association with unwanted conflict and intolerance.

- Instead of focusing on the inadequacies and perceived differences of the world religions, believers and non-believers alike can rally around the *universal values* of compassion, integrity, responsibility, and service.

- With these shared values as a foundation, individuals can empower themselves through the creation and *cultivation of gardens* showcasing their innate talents while leaving behind a lasting *legacy* and bettering those who cross their paths.

Next Destination

In Chapter 10, an old friend comes to visit to remind me of my humanity, and I unveil the road map to power drawn from the lessons learned throughout the book.

10

The Road Map to Power

Rule of the Road: Be more than humane; be a humanitarian.

If I were asked when the beginning of my journey to redefine and re-claim my power took place, I would point to the instant I climbed into Bob Anderson's sweltering car. If asked to determine the end, well, that's a harder question. My son and I were well on our way to putting pen to paper writing this book before I had a precise idea of its conclusion. The answer finally arrived, however (like many revelations we experience) while I was busy living my life.

I was preparing for our annual International Center for Psychosocial Trauma (ICPT)/International Medical and Educational Trust (IMET) con-ference designed for mental health professionals across the world to re-ceive training and share ideas on how to best treat the effects of trauma experienced by their clients. The week-long course culminates in a cele-bration banquet honoring a person who tirelessly strives to better the lives of those most in need. This distinction is aptly named the Humanitarian Award. Every year, the Board of ICPT/IMET and I comb over a list of wor-thy candidates ranging from well-known dignitaries to more under-the-radar, local heroes. Great effort is dedicated to vetting nominees properly. I was in the midst of several consecutive hours of review when I felt my eyes starting to tire. I took off my glasses, rubbed my eyes and brow, and sipped from a bottle of water. I put my glasses back on and was about to pore over the names once again when it became perfectly clear who should receive the award. The person wasn't on my carefully crafted list. She wasn't even a mental health professional. I laughed at the sheer obviousness of the answer and shook my head that it had taken me so long to come to this conclusion. After all, she had been with me since the beginning of ICPT/IMET.

Elma Dizdar came into my life when I was already in my 50s. While she came late to the game, her appearance would make an immediate impression, and this mutual connection would transfer to our entire family. She calls me Father. She calls my wife Mother. My two sons call her Sister despite the lack of legal recognition of this relationship. Neither a holiday nor a birthday celebration goes by without a call from across the ocean from our beloved Elma.

The account of how Elma earned the affection of the entire Husain family is nothing short of remarkable. In fact, I was never supposed to meet her. In February 1994, I visited the besieged city of Sarajevo to train teachers in trauma psychology and was in desperate need of an interpreter. Months before I arrived, a seasoned interpreter was arranged to bridge any language divides likely to occur during the seminars on treating post-traumatic stress disorder I and my mental health team had prepared for the Bosnian people. She reluctantly withdrew, however, because her husband was lost to enemy fire only a few days before our arrival. The subject matter would be too grueling for a grieving widow. Elma was the last-minute replacement. A native of Sarajevo, Elma was uniquely qualified for a job that tragedy dictated her to fill. She was a student of English and Arabic with a command of both languages and an astonishing memory, an occupational necessity in an arena where long dialogues and frequent interruptions are the norm. Elma's interpretation would include not only the words but also the gestures and emotions that accompanied them. Elma frowned or pointed at the same point in the narrative as the presenters did. If one of the presenters cried—there were many tears shed—Elma cried, too.

After the first session, critical in developing trust with the participants, Elma confided in me that she was coping with her own tragedy. Her 25-year-old cousin had been killed by a shell detonation the month before. About a year before, her uncle and her niece had been fatally shot by a sniper. Elma was haunted by the fear that something ominous was going to happen again. She was afraid she might lose another loved one and, eventually, her own life. This constant feeling of impending doom propels a person into a state of utter hopelessness and creates an attitude that nothing is worth the effort because no future exists. A few days before our arrival, she found herself surrounded by people full of enthusiasm, exclaiming that the experts from the U.S.A. were coming to help. She didn't believe a word of it. She had heard such promises before. When the seminar started, however, she found herself doing whatever she could to ensure its success. She told me, "Suddenly, it felt as if all of us were thrown into some twilight zone. Suddenly, things started to matter again. It was very important to work and get things done. It was so important that we stopped wondering if we were going to live long enough to see the results. It made sense to put on our makeup and nice clothes, though it made no sense at all."

Elma had rediscovered her courage. I say rediscovered because courage was not new to Elma when war broke out and ravaged her home. She was born with Tetralogy of Fallot, a set of four congenital heart defects, a combination that is almost always fatal. At the tender age of three, she had undergone extensive surgeries and later was fitted with a pacemaker. Perhaps it was this early experience that gave her the bravery she would need to crisscross a war zone to carry out her essential role as interpreter. Elma realized our level of dependency on her to complete each training seminar. Without interpretation, the material the mental health team presented in English would be useless to almost all of the participants. She became our ears and our tongue. Elma became a firm believer that this work was instrumental in improving the lives of the local children, and she was determined to make her way from Sarajevo to each seminar site regardless of personal risk.

To truly understand these risks, it is necessary to be familiar with "the tunnel." Constructed entirely by hand and dug out of raw earth, the tunnel became a lifesaving link to the outside world and a conduit for supplies. The Serb aggressors knew of the existence of the tunnel but not the exact location of its entrance. To access the tunnel, one had to crawl through a broken window into a deserted house. The tunnel itself was only about four feet wide, five feet high, and constituted the most agonizing 760-meter (half-mile) walk of your life. The tunnel was so narrow that two-way traffic was impossible. Travelers were required to wait outside while oncoming traffic cleared.

Elma went through the tunnel six times in order to interpret for the seminars. On one of her last journeys, she was followed by a friendly soldier. He took some joy in watching Elma try to navigate not only herself but also a suitcase full of critical materials through this absurdly narrow passage. His laughter stopped abruptly, however, when they emerged at the end. A shell had exploded only a few minutes earlier, and there were several visible casualties. People pushed their way through the crowd to escape, and the soldier pleaded for Elma to flee. His sense of urgency was fueled by the knowledge of his enemy's strategy to fire upon survivors attempting to help the wounded. Elma thanked the soldier for his concern while she proceeded forward into the chaos, an act of higher duty trumping the urge for self-preservation.

When the war was finally settled, Elma's importance to ICPT continued. She coordinated the follow-up of our research of 791 children from several elementary schools in Sarajevo, which was aimed at finding out how they were progressing after the initial interventions. She also became a vital player in future workshops designed to apply the lesson learned in Bosnia to other countries experiencing similar fates. Fortunately, this role allowed her the opportunity to come to the United States several times. It was during these trips that her combination of charisma and compassion endeared herself to our entire family and that she added the honorary title of our daughter and sister.

My suggestion to award Elma Dizdar the ICPT/IMET 15th Annual Humanitarian Award for her past and current service in aiding in the restoration of hope and healing of the Bosnian children was met with universal enthusiasm. Such was her reputation among my colleagues that she accepted the honor in front of a packed ballroom in Columbia, Missouri. Her name was called, and she quietly walked up to the podium and carefully surveyed the diverse crowd. For the next few minutes, the room full of professionals with important degrees sat still in a trance. I could attempt to summarize her words for you but would be guilty of a great disservice. So, instead, I present a large excerpt from her speech:

I must admit that, if asked to describe myself with a few words, I would not use the word "humanitarian" as one of them. Although helping people in need is a part of my nature, a part of my identity, of who I am, I would probably not describe myself as a humanitarian. It is because I understand the word humanitarian as describing persons going out of their way and making great sacrifices in their own lives in order to help others in need.

Having lived in a war zone, surrounded and immersed in human distress, just like anyone else living through another kind of disaster, I did not have to risk much in order to help. Only my own life, which all of us risked, anyway. to fetch water, go to work, take an exam, do just about anything.

Living in these circumstances, one has a duty to help. It is a humane thing to do, it is what one must do in order to be able to define himself or herself as a human being. It is for this reason that I would describe what I have done as a "humane" and not "humanitarian" action.

I decided to emphasize this for I know too well that for all the amazing people who have travelled with the ICPT, putting their lives in harm's way, risking never seeing their families again, risking the happy childhood of their own children in order to bring at least a ray of happiness to childhoods of distressed children around the world ... for all of them it would have been way too easy to stay at their homes, stay safe, stay warm, and while enjoying all the luxuries of the civilized life, contemplate in the cozy atmosphere of their living rooms how difficult it would be to do anything to help people who are so far away, cut off from the civilized world, impossible to reach. I myself as a survivor of a bloody war and fourteen hundred and twenty-five days of the longest siege in the history of mankind, as a person that was within days deprived of all the facets of the civilized life, a person who had to live second after second after second in fear that the next second might be my last, I have the greatest admiration for people like Dr. Husain and his team, who were willing to abandon the safety of their peaceful lives, the love of their families, the comfort of enjoying electricity, running water, and food safe enough to eat in order to travel where no one else thought of travelling to and bring light to people who already started losing hope that they would see the light of humanity again. They, in my view, are true humanitarians.

It is this thinking about the meaning of words, the meaning of "humane" and "humanitarian" that prompted me to discuss two very important ways in which language influences our lives. Being a linguist, I tend to see the power of language everywhere.

One of the things that linguistics and philosophy of language teach us is that it is language that actually defines what our world consists of. For us, what exists and what is the part of the world as we know it is what is spoken about or written about. Whole worlds could exist within our world without us being aware of them if they are not spelled out through language. This immense power of language over our lives is what we can suffer because of or benefit from. And it is up to us to decide in what way this power will affect our lives.

If we have a look at the history of mankind, it does not take long to understand that the way in which it is written, its content that is spelled out in language, makes it a history of conflicts, of wars, of struggle to balance powers, wherein the power is necessarily measured by the aggressive and violent potential of one society striking against the other, rather than the benevolent potential of one society helping the other. It seems to be in our human nature to give much more attention to destruction than to construction, to talk much more about violence and death than benevolence and saving lives. This is probably so because we perceive violence as something out of the ordinary—it in itself is news, whereas a human willingness to help is a part of the ordinary and it goes without saying. The explanation sounds very good when put in words, but in effect what this tendency does is paint the world in very dark tones without bringing in the light at all.

It is for this reason that we have to be aware that it is not only the helping efforts, but very importantly their visibility, that has the potential of changing the world. It is true that violence has the potential to do irreversible damage within seconds, whereas relief and helping efforts invariably take very long to make a positive difference. It has always been true that destruction is much easier and takes by far less time than construction or reconstruction. Still, we must not underestimate the power of the human heart. We must not forget how much hope and light an act of humanity can instill in lives of millions of people and how many millions of those more fortunate will be moved by our action and stand up to join us.

I have watched a video of this speech many times in a fleeting attempt to recapture the euphoria I first felt while experiencing it in person. The camera shows that once Elma finished with the phrase "stand up and join us," there is a brief silence. It is as if the people in attendance were taking a moment for her words to wash over them. Then, there is a spontaneous rising from the chairs and a shower of applause as if the crowd were unanimously saying, "Yes, we will stand up and join you." Every person was compelled to leave his or her seat to express pure gratitude and delight.

Elma's extraordinary words were important to me on a number of fronts. On the one hand, to see your daughter deliver a rhetorical masterpiece in front of your colleagues filled this father with pride. More important, she inspired the best in the trauma field to continue their essential work with the most in need. Long after the tablecloths were cleared and the banquet chairs put away, Elma's speech provided another function. It served as the ideal capstone to the Road Map to Power. What she was able to capture was where this quest to reclaiming personal power had taken me and why I had embarked on it in the first place.

My parents left the country of my birth for Pakistan because they were uncertain about the prospects that might be offered to their Muslim children after the 1947 Partition of India.[66] In Pakistan, we soon discovered that the manner in which the nation was politically structured, from the local principalities to the national level, would never afford me the opportunities I could pursue elsewhere. Once I had established myself in the United States, however, I fell into a different kind of trap prevalent in a consumer-oriented society. To demonstrate power, I believed I needed to be the possessor of things. The car ride with Bob brought to the surface what I was afraid to admit: I had essentially traded one power drain for another.

Elma's speech reaffirmed that although Bob technically dropped me off at my home, the car ride never stopped. The new path I decided to forge, summarized in upcoming pages as the road map to power, was like any trip you take. You have step-by-step directions to follow. You make stops along the way. You may even allow yourself a detour or two. Every step completed, however, gets you a little closer to your destination. To construct a new road map to power, I first had to determine where and why I had gone in the wrong direction. This deconstruction begins with the first rule in following the road map. We are likely average, mathematically speaking, an acknowledgment of my simple existence.

One of the byproducts of being born into or living in a first-world, individualistic society, is that we are taught that we are unique and special. As a child psychiatrist, I strongly advocate for parents to promote positive self-esteem in their children. As a doting grandfather, when I stare into the eyes of my grandson and granddaughter, I am convinced they are unique and special. No one, certainly not me, will begrudge a grandparent for this belief. The overvaluation of our significance, however, occurs when this personal appraisal is transcribed into universal terms. Our time on earth is but a flicker of light, our accomplishments fleeting, and our replacements readily available. In our quest to prove we are special, we forget how irrelevant we truly are.

The fact of the matter is whatever trait is being measured, we are basically data points positioned up and down the slopes of the bell curve. There will always be someone smarter, faster, stronger, taller, skinnier, and better looking.

Differences in these human traits are oftentimes subtle. Because some-one is stronger does not mean you are not strong, and it does not mean

---

66   Soon after the British Colonial exit from India, the country was divided into what is now known as India, Pakistan, and Bangladesh.

your strength is without value. Where the problem occurs is that the members of the 99% have failed to realize the rules of power have changed since we have become more Wal-Mart than wildebeest. To our ancestors, every asset, in large or small doses, had merit as long as it contributed to the survival of the group. The individual who could bear more weight may have received more adulation, but those who were able to carry their fair share also had worth. As human beings further mastered their environment, longevity became less earned and more of a birthright. Tribes became less nomadic, and permanent civilizations took root. Some skills were deemed more valuable, and the formation of class distinction began. Those with access to the echelon of the higher classes were able to accumulate power and wealth. Power was no longer an equation directly linked to the amount one contributed to the well-being of the whole.

In the world of Wal-Mart, i.e., a society in which almost every conceivable human need can be found in a store or one click away, the relationship between degree in which you exhibit a trait and what its worth is perceived to be does not follow a normal bell-curve distribution. Instead, wealth as a function of worth is distributed along a Pareto curve: The vast majority of wealth is concentrated on a select few individuals, leaving the masses to divvy up the leftovers. Those in a position to capitalize on this power dynamic are the ones who demonstrate biological endowment, are the inheritor of someone else's wealth, and/or are plain lucky. Unfortunately, all three of these pathways are almost entirely out of our personal control. We have no say over our genetics (at least not yet), we can't just conjure up a rich uncle, and they call it luck for a reason.

Still, despite the overwhelming statistical evidence proving otherwise, we blindly pursue power through these almost unreachable means. Part of this irrational behavior is entrenched in the themes and myths of our society. One of the best celebrated and most coveted documents of human history is what Thomas Jefferson penned: the Declaration of Independence. In its words, one can find the inspiration that drove the United States to become the most powerful and economically dominant nation in the world. The 99% would do well to remember, however, that when you get to the part about "created equal," keep reading. The promise of equality creates an illusion that we are all born with the same opportunity to succeed and that if we all put in an equal amount of hard work, then we will all arrive at the same destination.

The real kicker here is that the intent of the "created equal" passage was not to suggest we are somehow the same. It was the aspiration of a fledging nation to establish a society where no people would be denied their potential or the fruits of their labor based on the status or circumstance in which they were born. The United States, along with every country that has attempted similar social experiments, has struggled to adhere to this promise. People of color, women, immigrants, those born into poverty, those who ascribe to a certain religion, and those who are of a particular sexual orientation can provide ample evidence of this fact. Any shortcomings in this pledge for equality do not undermine the tremendous effort and strong will of those attempting to level the playing field. The rights of its citizens, even those eligible to become voting citizens, have increased tenfold since the ink dried on the American Constitution. This result is no small accomplishment and is built on the sweat and tears of many great people. No matter how egalitarian and enlightened a society becomes, however, no matter how progressive their policies are crafted, there will still be a gap between the haves and have-nots if power is defined as a derivative of the amount of wealth and resources acquired. For at the end of the day, governments cannot legislate genetics. The brain capacity of Stephen Hawking, the agility of Serena Williams, and the beauty of Jennifer Lawrence will always give them a leg up over the 99%. To their credit, they have maximized this advantage.

What is fascinating about our society is the skills both most revered and promoted are the ones least likely to provide any sustenance for those who dedicate time and energy to mastering them. When I ask young people what they want to be when they grow up, the most popular answers are athlete, musician, astronaut, artist, marine biologist (yes, this is popular), crime scene investigator (thank you, CSI), millionaire entrepreneur, doctor, lawyer, and an important politician (most often, president). All of these careers, some more than others, are heavy long shots. Each require a genetic threshold, be it physical or mental, that only a few possess. We cannot ignore the fact that we will all hit our biological ceiling, and we must be prepared when that moment arrives. This is not to say dreams should be discouraged or talents should be wasted. No, they must be cultivated and supported by family members and teachers. Who among us can say or predict which child has greatness inside them? A just and fair society ensures that this greatness can equally come from a penthouse in Manhattan or the rural mountains of Kentucky. It does not promise, however, that we will all get there. In fact, most of us won't.

The myth of equal opportunity and the false expectation that government can completely level the playing field only explains a portion of why the 99% fall prey to the allure of power through means almost exclusively reserved for the biologically and environmentally endowed. To fully comprehend our susceptibility to emulate the 1%, we have to begin at the moment we inhale our first breath of air. The doctor catches the baby, the umbilical cord is cut, and the newly arrived boy or girl is delivered to her delighted mother. Completely vulnerable, the child relies on those around to provide nourishment and safety. The primary caregiver is tasked with the bulk of this incredible responsibility. Done successfully, the child will likely learn to trust others, form meaningful relationships, and navigate his or her environment. The building block for this desirable result is known as a secure attachment, and it is the basis for rule number 5 in the road map to power: Looking for security? It's in the attachment.

Unfortunately, not all children are raised in a nurturing and supportive environment. These young boys and girls begin to view the world as harsh and unpredictable. They become distrustful of others, particularly adults, and often suffer from low self-esteem and even self-loathing. They also begin to look outside of themselves for satisfaction, making them particularly vulnerable to the accumulation of material possessions to fulfill self-esteem needs. Because they are never able to move past the emotional development of a child, an expensive car turns into a security object for them, much like a blanket or teddy bear is to a two-year-old. Of course, any positive feelings associated with this object are fleeting, and more cars, motorcycles, electronics, clothes, and jewelry are acquired in a losing attempt to fill this void.

The 99% should not feel ashamed or guilty for competing in this unwinnable game. On the contrary, those who refuse to play are demonstrating remarkable fortitude and self-control. Every day, we are inundated with messages from the media that remind us that we are not smart enough, good looking enough, or successful enough. Companies employ teams of people and spend billions of dollars in an attempt to exploit any feelings of insecurity or need to socially compare. As society and technology has rapidly progressed, the tools available are increasingly more pervasive and sophisticated. Movies, television, radio, the Internet, social media, and the roads we drive are saturated with advertisements that promise to make us smarter, more attractive, and more popular. Even what we wear has turned each one of us into a walking billboard.

Thankfully, there is good news because chances are you're happy despite the best efforts of the media. As mentioned earlier, researchers at Princeton University have shown that the amount of money a family needs to earn to feel the same emotional well-being as a multimillionaire is much lower than one would expect, the aforementioned $75,000 breakeven point. Where one finds the difference between the $75,000 earner and the super-rich is not in emotional well-being, but in life evaluation. Life evaluation is more concerned about whether a person believes they are advancing in the world as they hoped and if they are achieving the goals they've set forth. This variable is where companies strike gold through the media and advertisements. The belief that, "Yeah, I am happy; but if I had a little bit more, I would be happier," is what the 99% must guard against. This outcome is no small order. While we are busy living our lives, extremely talented and motivated people are targeting not only our needs but also, more predatorily, our weaknesses and vulnerabilities. Thus, to protect ourselves from the onslaught of negative and destructive messaging from the media and others who benefit from our tendency to socially compare, we must forge our armor out of resiliency.

Resiliency is the ability of an individual to bounce back from adversity and difficult circumstances. This quality is found in abundance in the children I have had the pleasure of working with who are surviving in war zones and disaster areas across the world. The expectation would be that these boys and girls would crumble, and yet a plurality are able to push onward, find means to survive, and keep the flame of hope burning.

What is strong enough to resist the worst of humankind is the ideal substance to shield ourselves from the harmful elements that exist in a modern and consumption-obsessed society. Best of all, and unlike most biological qualities that tend to favor only a select few, nature favors the building blocks for developing a resilient personality. The combination of temperaments most conducive in promoting resiliency also happens to be the most common in children. "Easy children" generally are able to adapt to their surroundings, remain confident in their problem-solving ability, and have an optimistic outlook on life.

Adults can play an important role in boosting core resiliency in all children regardless of temperament factors. The creation of supportive networks—from caring family members to mentor figures, from open neighborhoods to strong cultural and spiritual identities—form a deep reservoir of resources and go-to people when times become challenging. Thus, while your chances of raising a Nobel Prize recipient are slim, raising a resilient child is a strong bet.

Fortunately, most children will not be required to test their degree of resiliency in a war zone or be displaced due to natural disaster. Without diminishing the struggles of those individuals who were forced to face these extreme circumstances, it is important that the 99% understand that they are facing a different type of war. The battle raging on in every household is one aimed at your remaining slice of power. A battalion of people are willing to remove you from your most valuable assets—money, time and energy, and sense of self-worth and dignity—for their own personal gain. Imagine what it takes for someone to stand up and say, "I do not need what you are selling," whether that be a product or an idea, and respond with, "I am comfortable with who I am." This resolve necessitates a secure attachment, a positive self-esteem, and a healthy dose of resiliency.

A resilient person is one who believes that he or she controls his or her own destiny. A great conflict of modern society, however, is that despite a litany of freedoms and an infinite number of choices, many people feel as though they have no control over the direction of their life. It is the perception that outside forces are writing the pages of their past, present, and future. This helpless existence brings us to rule number 8 in the road map to power: If you don't like the ending, rewrite the story. Our personal narratives are often inherited from our parents and their parents before them. Themes of poverty or affluence, middle-class work ethic or criminal background, failure or success, race- or gender-related stereotypical expectations can dictate how we navigate the world and how others will perceive us.

I had assumed a narrative that had become counterproductive to the aims and goals of my life. I had authored a belief that being a prominent professional, the director of a large child mental health center, required the image of economic prosperity. This projection was based on the erroneous belief of what I thought people expected of me. Most damagingly, it left me exposed to the twin evils of materialism and overconsumption. I was concerned about where this story was leading me and how it might end. Thus, my journey following the road map of power required reclamation of my narrative.

A core tenet of narrative therapy is to dig deep into the stories of challenge and strife and mine elements of great strength and courage. I was able to extract from my own childhood and young adult life qualities and values for this process of re-authoring. I had been raised in an environment of humility and simplicity, one that stressed the importance of maintaining convictions and aiding those most in need. Despite meager assets, it was a time of great happiness and possibility. Now that resources were more abundant, I did not have to run away from this simplicity. In fact, doing so would be a denial of my core existence. Similarly, many individuals have given up on a reality more akin to their dreams and authentic self. We must remember that inside each of us is the capacity to override what people think we should be and author the narrative of who we hope to become. Striving for this ideal will not only generate increased benefits for yourself but also set up your future generations to reap the seeds of power that have been sowed.

Whether we are members of the 99% or have defied the odds with a seat at the banquet table of the 1%, we are all part of a common human narrative. This narrative is propelled by the two quintessential questions of the human condition: Why are we here, and how do we deal with our impending death? These concerns have inspired an endless stream of writing, artwork, and song. They have driven the most powerful people of their time to build, often on the backs of the poor and enslaved, mausoleums with the dual purpose of celebrating legacies and preparing for the life beyond.

The unquenchable thirst for answers to these questions has also spawned numerous religions and spiritual beliefs practiced by billions of people across the globe. Much of the focus has centered on the differences in these convictions, and war and violence of every kind has been blamed on one religion attempting to establish dominance over another. What is lost in this battle of supremacy is the good that also comes from practices of religion and spirituality. While conflict arises due to differences in faith, each major religion has espoused a remarkably similar value system. This code of ethics includes the promotion of compassion, integrity, responsibility, and service. In these commonalities—the ties that bind all human beings—an important power source emerges. Combining universal core values with the talents found inside each individual presents the opportunity for all of us to cultivate our gardens.

As a principal component of reclaiming my narrative, I decided to finally perform my first pilgrimage to Mecca to begin my new journey. Surrounded by men and women from disparate backgrounds, I experienced firsthand the singularity of the human spirit. I began to meditate on an especially powerful and universally resonating verse of the Qur'an:

"It is not righteous that you turn your face towards east or west, but it is righteousness to believe in God and the last day and angels and the book and the prophets, to spend of your wealth in spite of your love for it, do all you can for orphans, for the needy, for the wayfarer, of those who ask and

for the ransom of slaves, to be steadfast in prayer and practice regular charity to fulfill the contracts which you have made and to be firm and patient
in pain and adversity and throughout all years of panic such of the people
should be God minded" (Qur'an 2:177).

This awakening removed the cloud of uncertainty I experienced stepping out of Bill's car and replaced it with a clear direction forward. Blessed
with the necessary education, resources, and connections, unsaddled by
the burden of expending these assets in pursuit of false power, I was in a
unique position to help those most traumatized and displaced by disaster
both of natural and human creation.

Shortly afterward, my wife, Jennifer, and I became aware of the plight
of the Bosnian people. We were both outraged and heartbroken. When
Jennifer suggested I organize a trauma team to travel to the ravaged country, I could not dismiss this series of events as mere coincidence nor could
I ignore the obvious signs. With the preparations in place, the last task was
for my wife and I to sit down with my two sons to ask them for their approval. While they offered a definite "yes," they could not fully appreciate
the danger of this decision or ultimately, what they would be signing off on.
My wife, on the other hand, was all too aware of the consequences of allowing her husband and the father of her children to freely enter an active war
zone. Her consent was reflective of her own compassionate spirit, devoted
faith, and a sequence of support that began the moment she, a Catholic,
took a chance on a Muslim foreigner attempting to fashion an uncertain
future in an unknown land. As the first-born daughter of a Hall of Fame
football coach, possessing stunning natural beauty, and having a promising
career already in progress, she had a myriad of conduits to achieving her
own power. Instead of choosing a road of personal and public accolades,
she made the decision to devote her vocation to the raising of our sons and
her avocation to volunteer efforts for the betterment of our community's
environmental, educational, and recreational wellbeing. With the security
of our children in gifted hands, I was mentally and physically liberated to
pursue my convictions.

The consistent time away, not to mention the considerable financial
implications of this charitable work, would be a challenge to any spouse.
For Jennifer, however, the unwavering commitment to these important
causes was authentic to a woman who had already marched for civil
rights and would later spearhead both the annual fundraiser MS Dinner
of Champions and the Multiple Sclerosis Institute as well as help establish

a free medical clinic for the under- and uninsured in our hometown. In her example was the embodiment of the principles espoused throughout this book. Even today she serves as a critical component in my ability to navigate my road to power; a loving companion willing to travel every mile by my side.

With the blessings of my family secure, the ICPT team, first tested in Bosnia and later put to use in places as diverse as Palestine, Russia, Indonesia, and Joplin, Missouri, became my garden. It was the unification of a resiliency formed by my loving mother and father, a narrative of being a refugee camp survivor myself, and the tenets of a religion that teaches to give whatever you have to a person who asks even if he arrives on a horse.[67] Besides providing assistance and training in disaster areas, ICPT/IMET has led to the formation in Pakistan of a hospital for those unable to afford proper medical treatment and a cluster of elementary schools for boys and girls who otherwise would grow up without an education. These nonprofit organizations have also become a vehicle for some of the most talented mental health practitioners, physicians, and educators to showcase their considerable skills. They have become the groundskeepers of this garden and have allowed wondrous flowers to bloom.

Similarly, every member of the 99% has gifts to share with one another. These unique contributions can form the foundation for each person's garden. They must, however, extend beyond doing a good deed—what Elma referred to as a "duty to help." Assisting someone whose car is stuck in the snow, reuniting a lost child with her mother, or even donating to a local charity fall under this category of "duty to help." While these actions should never be taken for granted, the cultivation of our gardens requires transcending the "humane thing to do."

In this principle lies the final destination on the road map to power: *Be more than humane; be a humanitarian.* To achieve this outcome requires a persistent and unflinching commitment to the betterment of others. It means dedicating all available resources to this universal cause. It necessitates the abandonment of the desire for personal gain. The mistake the 99% make is to view their talents as a pathway to fame and fortune. Endowments both of the nature and nurture type become a financial equation in

---

67   A reference to a lesson shared by the Prophet Mohammad to his fellow Muslims imploring them to offer charity to whomever asks regardless of appearance. Travel by horse during the time of Mohammad was a sign of affluence and would call into question the rider's motivation for financial assistance; the modern equivalent of a person showing up in a Mercedes and requesting money to fill their gas tank.

which the addition of a skill or degree on one side of the equal sign leads to the increase of money on the other. Certainly, it is paramount to be paid for our work. Defining self-worth, however, as a product of monetary worth places the value of our abilities in the hands of only a select few. It is a boss, a number-crunching administrator, or a union representative charged with collective bargaining who will set our "deserved" rate. This evaluation will in most cases leave us feeling underappreciated and dissatisfied.

What if, instead, we looked at our talents not in terms of the profit to be gained but in how they can best benefit others? The value comes from the giving, a transaction that requires no approval from above and over which we have complete control and freedom. The rewards from this approach then begin to flow in abundance. For what may seem to be self-sacrifice, the individual who walks this road will be indulged with a lifetime of nourishment for the mind, body, and soul.

I am living proof. Every action in the cultivation of my garden has produced more fruit than any man deserves.

A noted gardener in his own right, St. Francis of Assisi stated, "It is in the giving that we receive." As a man of great conviction, St. Francis was speaking of rewards we receive not only in this life but in the hereafter. My faith tradition also speaks of a peaceful immortality gained by following a "straight path." By dedicating oneself to the service of others, by ascribing to a core philosophy of decency and integrity, a paradise awaits. No one, least of all me, can promise you what will happen when you die. What I can state clearly, however, is the road map is consistent with the values championed by the great religions of the world. For those adhering to and practicing these values, the glorious end result has been made abundantly clear.

I recognize not all believe in this eternal message. Road Map to Power is designed not to discriminate between those who have faith in a higher power and those who do not. In fact, the principles of the road map address the issues of immortality regardless of where one finds himself or herself on the question of divinity. Picture the warmth you feel witnessing the smile, the handshake, the look in someone's eye, the tears of joy, or the hug of someone expressing sincere gratitude. In that moment of giving, the best part of you lives on in the courage of another to confront whatever obstacles stand in the way. In turn, it inspires the receiver of your kindness to act likewise. This chain reaction of love can continue ad infinitum. It is in much the same way that those who have affected our lives continue to exist in our good works and deeds. We now have the opportunity: Our body may decay, yet the best piece of us can now reside in the hearts of thousands who remain to carry the torch of altruism and compassion.

To be a part of changing the dominant paradigm of taking recklessly to giving unconditionally is the essence of a renewable power for the future and one that will always leave you satisfied. That is the essence of power prescribed by this path.

Entering the twilight of my life, with so much more work left to do, I am eternally thankful that this straight path was laid before me. Not a morning goes by without me ruminating on the saying, "Every person has three days." The first day is of my parents. They have long been deceased, but they left me a treasure trove of kindness and wisdom to last me my lifetime. The second day is of me. I know, too, that I am staring into the setting horizon. The third day is of my children. To see my two sons choose to share their talents in the urban decay for an oft-forgotten people (one as a doctor, another as an educator) fills me with pride. I may never have a statue built in my honor or a building bearing my name, but to know that my children will continue the legacy of compassion set forth by my mother and father is a gift to me that can never be repaid. I will take that tradeoff any day.

In stating this fact, I know how dangerously close I was to going a different way. As a successful physician, I suppose no one would have faulted me for being pleased by my accomplishments and resting on my laurels. Despite my modest beginnings in Pakistan, I was able to provide food and clothing for my children, climb to the top of my profession without taking shortcuts, and manage to help some people around me along the way. However, something in me was not satisfied, like a thirst that could not be quenched. Then, Bob arrived in his beat-up car.

Experiencing Bob's story firsthand, my original instinct was to believe that in order to reclaim power lost over my life, I needed to shed myself of all exorbitant possessions. Bob sized up the society around him and realized that a middle-class mental health worker would be buried under unfulfilled expectations if he attempted to chase power through traditional means. His solution was to reject the conventional rules of consuming, borrowing, and lending. It meant less material possessions and delaying the gratification of a new home or car until sufficient savings were reached to purchase with cash. By adopting this philosophy, Bob owed no one, and, in turn, no one owned him.

The equation seemed clear to me: Power equaled minimalism. I was living and had been conditioned to believe, like most of the 99%, that power equals excess. Discarding this excess, however, was only the means and not the ends of Bob's personal calculus. What I failed to initially realize is the result of Bob's lifestyle that made him truly powerful: He was free to be an uncompromising humanitarian. After all, what is the point of simplicity if just to live simply? To harness the entirety of power belonging to his decision, it must be connected to the greater good. Thus, all of Bob's choices were dictated by what was best for his clients and those he served. Once he determined he was no longer in a position to operate under this mandate, he walked away. Given Bob's conventional status, he had to systemically relieve himself of the burdensome weight of material baggage to position himself to arrive at his acceptable resolution. Certainly, this course of action wasn't in his perceived best self-interest, but it allowed him to be authentic, true to his purpose, why he believed he was put on this earth ... why we are all put on this earth.

When I say "all," I mean everyone. Up to this point, we have looked at the road map as if it were two different routes, one that the 99% can travel and one on which only the 1% can tour in luxury. For all the feigning and fawning of the rich, for all the yearning and effort to be considered elite, the irony is that those who are fortunate enough to reach this destination often find themselves just as unfulfilled as those who fail to reach this summit. In other words, even if we were fortunate enough to ascend to the ranks of the 1%, there is no guarantee of increased happiness or sense of dignity.

Pope Francis, a leader committed to bringing the plight of the poor and marginalized into the spotlight, poignantly noted, "The worship of the golden calf of old has found a new and heartless image in the cult of money and the dictatorship of an economy which is faceless and lacking any truly human goal." Look at the struggles of the rich and famous in pursuit of this false goal. How many of them have taken their own lives? How many have spiraled into depression or spun out of control on a diet of drugs, booze, and excess? How many have left in their wake broken families and children resentful of their mother's or father's addiction to fame? These outcomes have become so commonplace that when we read the latest self-inflicted tragedy to befall a celebrity or powerful icon, we shrug it off as normal.

Now take a cue from some of the wealthiest individuals in the world who spent their time accumulating more money than their next ten generations could ever spend. What are they doing with all of their hard-earned currency? They are giving all of it away. Here is a small sample of well-known billionaires who have taken The Giving Pledge, an oath to distribute a vast amount of their wealth to foundations promoting positive human endeavors: Paul Allen, Ted Turner, Warren Buffet, Michael Bloomberg, Marc Zuckerberg, George Lucas, T. Boone Pickens, Bill and Melinda Gates, Larry Ellison, Richard and Joan Branson, and Richard Edwin and Nancy Peery Marriott. When the dust has settled, the dividends paid out, the assets tabulated, and the cash counted, the impossibly rich take stock of their lives in the same manner as any of us. Being a humanitarian, living to serve, just so happens to also be the final conclusion of the 1%.

Does this shift in thinking mean we are likely to see the members of the Fortune 500 take vows of poverty? Highly unlikely. Does it mean that their children won't be left a substantial inheritance? Of course not. Does it even open up the possibility that they take a page from Bob's playbook and limit the pleasures and conveniences of a modern society? A resounding no. And, really such questions and answers are beside the point. Of exclusive importance, The Giving Pledge is symbolic of the realization from the "captains' of industry" that their legacy and sense of fulfillment is directly tied to their altruistic influence on their communities.

Of course, advocating for a life of selflessness and the empowerment of others is by no means a revolutionary philosophy. It is a message that has been preached since antiquity and has been retold to the contemporary masses by some of the most revered women and men throughout time. If anything, Road Map to Power hopes to bring this way of life back to the forefront of conversation of the individual, the family, and society as a whole. Instead of just repackaging an age-old belief, the road map serves as proof how challenging it has become to arrive at what is seemingly a clear and simple destination. This fact is a great paradox of modern existence: Never before have there been so many people capable of making a profound difference and yet never have there been so many temptations to behave otherwise. This authentic road has been permeated with potholes, wrong turns, toll gates, and washed-out bridges. Yes, you may be patted on the back or told "good job" when you have done a kind deed, but the megaphone of our society screams at us to be different than who we are, to win at all cost, and to climb over those who stand in our way. This "me first" groundswell suggests to us that power is dominance, power is oppression, power is conquest. These destructive definitions lead us to, as Elma described, "paint the world in very dark tones without bringing in the light at all."

To steer clear of the emptiness such a pursuit brings and instead unlock the essence of real, lasting, and obtainable power by being a beacon of light for others, you will have to debunk the myths of a bloated consumer society and disregard the siren song of a viral media. You will have to stay resilient and surround yourself with individuals who support your seemingly unconventional choices. This path will require you to build a narrative that places at the centerpiece the themes and principles most critical to your life. It will mean putting yourself in the difficult position to walk away when you are inevitably asked to compromise your value system. You will be mandated to share your experience, education, and talents to improve the conditions of those most in need.

This road will not always be easy, but the accolades will be sincere, the feelings of satisfaction meaningful, and the impact will resonate beyond your lifetime. Most encouragingly, it will not require superior genetics, wealth, or luck for you to travel. In fact, it's available to all of us, equally.

Select MSI Books

Self-Help Books

A Woman's Guide to Self-Nurturing (Romer)

Creative Aging: A Baby Boomer's Guide to Successful Living (Vassiliadis & Romer)

Divorced! Survival Techniques for Singles over Forty (Romer)

How to Be a Good Mommy When You're Sick: A Guide to Motherhood with Chronic Illness (Graves)

Lessons of Labor: One Woman's Self-Discovery through Labor and Motherhood (Aziz)

Living Well with Chronic Illness (Charnas)

Publishing for Smarties: Finding a Publisher (Ham)

The Marriage Whisperer: How to Improve Your Relationship Overnight (Pickett)

The Rose and the Sword: How to Balance Your Feminine and Masculine Energies (Bach & Hucknall)

The Widower's Guide to a New Life (Romer)

Widow: A Survival Guide for the First Year (Romer)

Inspirational and Religious Books

A Believer-Waiting's First Encounters with God (Mahlou)

A Guide to Bliss: Transforming Your Life through Mind Expansion (Tubali)

El Poder de lo Transpersonal (Ustman)

Everybody's Little Book of Everyday Prayers (MacGregor)

Joshuanism (Tosto)

Puertas a la Eternidad (Ustman)

The Gospel of Damacus (O. Imady)

The Seven Wisdoms of Life: A Journey into the Chakras (Tubali)

When You're Shoved from the Right, Look to Your Left: Metaphors of Islamic Humanism (O. Imady)

Memoirs

Blest Atheist (Mahlou)

Forget the Goal, the Journey Counts . . . 71 Jobs Later (Stites)

Healing from Incest: Intimate Conversations with My Therapist (Henderson & Emerton)

It Only Hurts When I Can't Run: One Girl's Story (Parker)

Las Historias de Mi Vida (Ustman)

Losing My Voice and Finding Another (C. Thompson)

Of God, Rattlesnakes, and Okra (Easterling)

Road to Damascus (E. Imady)

Foreign Culture

Syrian Folktales (M. Imady)

The Rise and Fall of Muslim Civil Society (O. Imady)

Thoughts without a Title (Henderson)

Psychology/Philosophy

Understanding the People around You: An Introduction to Socionics (Filatova)

Humor

Mommy Poisoned Our House Guest (C. B. Leaver)

The Musings of a Carolina Yankee (Amidon)

Other

365 Teacher Secrets for Parents: Fun Ways to Help Your Child in Elementary School (McKinley & Trombly)

The Subversive Utopia: Louis Kahn and the Question of National Jewish Style in Jerusalem (Sakr)

CPSIA information can be obtained
at www.ICGtesting.com
Printed in the USA
FSOW04n0523051015
11767FS